the year of knots

WINDY CHIEN

ABRAMS, NEW YORK

editor: shawna mullen
designer: heesang lee
production manager: kathleen gaffney

library of congress control number: 2018958267

isbn: 978-1-4197-3280-5
eisbn: 978-1-68335-667-7

printed and bound in china

10 9 8 7 6 5 4 3

abrams books are available at special discounts when purchased in quantity
for premiums and promotions as well as fundraising or educational use.
special editions can also be created to specification. for details, contact
specialsales@abramsbooks.com or the address below.

abrams® is a registered trademark of harry n. abrams, inc.

ABRAMS The Art of Books
195 Broadway, New York, NY 10007
abramsbooks.com

—

"[The] simple act of tying a knot is an adventure in unlimited space . . . an excursion that is limited only by the scope of our own imagery and the length of the rope maker's coil."

CLIFFORD ASHLEY, *The Ashley Book of Knots*

introduction 6

about the knots in this book 8

introduction

On January 4, 2016, I was at home in San Francisco in my backyard woodworking shed, sweeping up sawdust, aware of the new year ahead. I wondered, idly, what it might bring. What happened next—in a flash—was completely unexpected by me at that moment in time: I had an actual "lightbulb moment," the kind I thought happened only in fiction. In the space of seconds, an entire year of knots laid itself out to me. Yes, knots. As in rope, tied.

At that time, I was a couple of years into my creative search after leaving my career at Apple. I had a small income from hand-carved wood spoons, "brass knuckle" rings, and a knotted pendant lamp I had named the Helix Light that was fast becoming popular with interior designers. Of all my projects, I was most compelled by macramé, but I was beginning to suspect the traditional form's limitations might be a creative dead end. I certainly had no idea it would lead me to this revelation.

The year 2016 unfurled itself in my mind as I swept: **I would learn one new knot each and every day of the year.** I would post the daily results on Instagram, not only to keep myself accountable, but as a reference and a record. I would include captions explaining the knots' names, histories, and utility, so that others could learn alongside me. I had no idea then *if* others would be interested, but I hoped they might be. I instantly intuited the project's self-imposed design constraints, such as making the knots out of white rope and photographing them on a white background, for visual consistency and in order to emphasize what I find to be the most compelling element of the art of knot-making: the line.

On that day, to catch up to the calendar, I learned and made four knots. I had 362 to go after that, because 2016 was a leap year—in more ways than one, as I would very soon discover.

What a leap indeed! I didn't know that within one year, I would present my work to museum curators, travel the country installing knot art on a majestic floor-to-ceiling scale, and secure my first gallery show. I didn't know then that my social media following would increase tenfold (and counting) and that I would be featured by *Wired*, *Martha Stewart Living*, the *New York Times*, and the *San Francisco Chronicle*. I didn't know that I would end up with a wall-size installation of more than three hundred unique knots that holds its own as a single work of art. I didn't know that within one short year I'd have discovered, developed, and honed my own creative process and voice.

I didn't know that I would begin writing my first book.

Knot by knot, day by day, I changed my life. And if I can change my life, so can you.

about the knots in this book

My earliest association with knots was my mother teaching me to make a macramé plant hanger when I was a kid in West Point, New York. Macramé was trendy then and it was a craft you could do at home. And Mom wasn't shy: We made a supersize, two-tiered plant hanger, probably out of a *Sunset* magazine. I loved the process intensely; it was an early formative experience for me.

The next time knots came into my consciousness, I was in my early twenties, thrifting in San Francisco, as we all did. I came across a how-to book of knots, which obviously struck a chord, so I purchased it without much thought. It wasn't beautiful—it was a manual—but I had to have it. You know how it is: Owning a book about something cool is like owning a little bit of that coolness. It makes you think you're cool, too, even if you're not actually doing the thing in the book! At most, I had a vague sense that, come a rainy day, I'd learn some of the knots.

Today, I have many knotting books in my library. Some are encyclopedias attempting to document the entirety of known knots (there are thousands). Others cover subsets of the knotting world based on function, occupation, or cultural origin. For example, China, Korea, and Japan have rich ornamental knotting traditions. One of my favorite books is by famed tightrope walker Philippe Petit, whose cutely titled book *Why Knot?* is filled with the knots that preserve his life when he performs death-defying feats.

All these reference tomes have their place and are useful. When I appear in public to present my work, the majority of people who approach me to speak are sailors and climbers who have those same books. These folks depend on knots' utility and reliability.

But I have come to realize that the reason I love knots is different from other knotters' reasons. I love those very same handy, practical knots not only for their usefulness, but also because they're beautiful.

Sure, **knots are little miracles of science.** They're ingeniously engineered, hardworking objects: What is the direction of pull? Where does the tension lie? How many cords make up the knot—one, two . . . eight? How strong is it, how secure is it (a different thing entirely), and what is its function? I see these empirical qualities as a feat of design, and when you look at it that way, you begin to see knots as singular expressions stationed at the intersection of science and aesthetics.

Clifford Ashley, who authored one of the definitive knot books (and my personal bible), *The Ashley Book of Knots*, defines a knot as "any complication in a length of line." A concise definition, to be sure, but it's also fantastically poetic, and reminds me of how Tom Waits speaks about music as doing interesting things to the air.

I feel exactly the same way about knots. Start with a straight line and bend it into a slight curve: This is a bight. Overlap the line onto itself and you have a loop. Add more complications and you have the beginnings of any one of several knot families. In every knot, the line will enter, travel around itself, other strands, or objects, then emerge from the knot. *The line charts a journey.*

I have always believed that famous line about the eye needing to travel. Although it came from a fashion editor, to me it gets at the human desire for stories.

If a knot is a complication in a length of line, perhaps life is similar: a journey filled with opportunity, in the story we write for ourselves.

For this book, I've chosen to teach my favorite knots—the ones I find myself using most often, some I invented, some that are just plain fun, and some that have become building blocks on which I've based entire bodies of work. I've made sure to include knots from most of the major knot families, so you'll find simple workhorse knots that come in handy in a variety of situations, many delightful decorative knots, and knots that tell you what they want to become and how they want to be used only after you've made them.

Learn the knots in the order in which they appear, as they build in complexity. My goal is to get your hands busy, but I don't necessarily expect you to become a professional knotter. Rather, my hope is that this book will help and inspire you to embark on *your own* creative path, whatever that may be.

So, dear reader, consider this book an idiosyncratic introduction to my aesthetic; a narrative of the paths traced by my curiosity; and merely the first step on your own journey of discovery.

giving myself permission

I n my life, I've given myself permission to make big changes three times. I tell you these stories not only to illustrate the leaps I made, but also to encourage you to consider what's possible for yourself. The first time, I gave myself permission to leave my identity. The second time, I let go of financial security. **The third time I gave myself permission, it was to prioritize my creativity above all else.**

That's why I often say I'm now on my third life. By the time the Year of Knots was born, I had already lived two of them.

After studying film in college, I spent fourteen years in the music industry, operating and then owning the independent San Francisco record shop Aquarius Records. There, my staff and I evangelized the music we loved, from punk to indie rock, Ethiopian jazz to Norwegian black metal, Jamaican rocksteady to Brazilian Tropicália.

Aquarius opened in 1969 and it was already legendary when I came on a couple of decades later. The Dead Kennedys met

there. Hüsker Dü played an in-store in our backyard. A member of the famously anonymous art band the Residents had worked at Aquarius. The scene I was part of was driven by the DIY ethos. We were one of a handful of small, independent record stores that made things happen, and were known throughout the world. (Rough Trade in England and Other Music in New York are other examples from the day.)

In 1996, I moved Aquarius to the Mission District's Valencia Street, which today is arguably "the hippest street in America" (I only say that because I've been reading it for the past ten years). How did I do it? The original owner wasn't interested in the move, so I asked him to sell the store to me. I borrowed $25,000 from two of my best customers and that was that. At the time, the Mission had moved on from its Irish roots to housing Latino immigrants, artists, and a healthy population of San Francisco freaks of the nineties, i.e., our customer base. It's where my staff and my customers lived, and it was just one step ahead of what became the first mass wave of dot-com gentrification, and the tech boom. Moving the shop to the Mission just made sense at the time. Little did I know it would become one of the most coveted retail locations in the city.

In the independent music industry, to be a badass, there are three things you can do. 1. Be in an awesome band. 2. Start your own label. 3. Own a record store. I chose number 3, and over the course of fourteen years, I befriended my musician heroes, produced concerts and festivals, toured with Lollapalooza, lived ten times the life many people get to, contributed to the worldwide music scene, all of it.

The act of building community and providing a space for good music to thrive was enormously satisfying, but after doing it for so long, I was increasingly curious about how the rest of the world lived. **If you're like me, you're omnivorous about life—you want to experience all it has to offer.**

The challenge was leaving my identity. My identity—indeed, almost two decades of my life—was wrapped up in being "Windy from Aquarius." My boho, Mission it-girl, indie-music identity. That might sound silly now, but the identity you cultivate in your twenties is your first adult *you*. That's when you express not only what you care about, but also who you want to be. And it becomes your personal brand. So, in order to leave the record shop, I had to give myself permission to leave my identity.

When I sold the record store, as part of the deal, I negotiated a year's worth of monthly payments to provide some space and security to figure out my future. I had no idea what I wanted to do next, but I'm not ashamed of that. In fact, you may be at the same crossroads, but a modicum of careful planning will allow you not to let the unknown hold you back. I think it's unrealistic to expect yourself to really, really know what you're going to do next

when you're working full-time. It's best to give yourself time to explore.

The next big move turned out to be Apple. I had always considered working at a record store to be my dream job. No one was more surprised than I when my only other imagined dream job came into view. I had been utterly captivated by Apple products since my father brought home an Apple IIe when I was a high school sophomore. I learned to program in BASIC and was in my high school computer club. By 2005, I had owned almost every iteration of Apple product, and I found the operating system so thoughtfully designed and usable that I was a superfan. When Apple released iTunes, which was the storefront to purchase digital music, plenty of people from my former life were incensed. The notion of music online, music without liner notes and record sleeves, not to mention the whole tech thing, was a big "no" from my erstwhile compatriots. But I never felt that way. I've always been format-agnostic. It's always been about the music and the musicians who make it, not the mode of delivery.

My first gig there was producing iTunes Essentials, which was basically a new version of a mixtape; then I moved on to larger campaigns, such as the annual "best of the year" celebration and big brand partnership promotions.

I was there for five years of explosive growth before moving to the App Store to manage editorial for three years. Curating apps instead of music felt fresh, and I regarded app and game designers as incredibly creative pioneers at the forefront of what the new mobile, touchscreen interface could be.

I loved working for a company whose mission and products I believed in. But after eight years, **I noticed I was spending a lot of time gazing longingly at the work of makers of tangible objects,** whose images scrolled across my screen each day while I toiled on a computer keyboard. I was so envious. And the fatigue of working at a large corporation had begun to erode my satisfaction. Additionally— and this is something to pay attention to if it is happening to you, too—I realized I had spent my careers at both the record store and Apple supporting the creativity of *other* people. **I longed to focus on my own creativity . . . and felt (and you should, too, no matter where you work) that I had earned the right to do so.**

Once I decided to make a change, I prepared to move on. I had already given myself permission to leave the identity I'd had at the record store, and so my next challenge became this: how to give myself permission to forgo financial security while I sought my next life.

Obviously, financial security is a big deal. I come from a middle-class family of immigrants. My dad and brother joined the US military. I had worked while putting myself through college, and the record store was a labor of love that had never brought in much money. In short: I didn't feel like I could afford to throw money around. But, I knew my heart wasn't in it anymore. And it's not right to cling to a job you don't love. To paraphrase Steve Jobs, your work is a big part of your life, so the only way to be happy is to do great work—and **the only way to do great work is to truly love what you do.** Don't settle for less.

Your boss is never going to invite you to leave your job. Your parents are never going to say, "Why don't you stop collecting that paycheck?" **So, if no one's ever going to give you permission, you just have to be comfortable with giving it to yourself.**

So I gave myself permission again, this time to leave the very real security of success and a paycheck. I knew that had I stayed, finances would never be a concern. When I told my risk-averse Chinese parents I was leaving this plum position, I could have lost their approval. Was I scared? Sure, a little, because I didn't know what was next. But remember, I had had good fortune with my prior decision to leave the record store, which had led me to another incredible mini lifetime. I was confident that I could do it again because I had done it once before.

And then, freed from corporate life, **I gave myself permission to prioritize my creativity.** But I don't regret my "desk job" years for a single minute, and you shouldn't, either. Wherever you are in life, I suggest you regard all your cumulative experiences as part of what make up your unique point of view, which will serve you so well on your creative path. For me, I was delighted to discover that the years of honing my taste by looking at, loving, and evangelizing *other* people's work actually came in handy when I started making art. Today, I am able to very quickly get to the heart of what I do (or don't) love about something I'm working on, and in which direction to go next. I absolutely believe that spending so many years focusing on others' art gave me the clarity and the ability to quickly develop my own.

knots& bolts

Read the instructions first.

In this book's tutorials, I've broken down the knot-tying process into as many simple steps as possible. Still, like you would for a cookbook recipe, read all the instructions for each knot before attempting.

Work, don't yank.

Never yank an end to attempt to draw a knot together all at once. Most knots must be gently "worked" bit by bit, section by section, usually starting from the center and moving outward. This way, the knot will retain its shape rather than distort or jam. This may be a slow process when you are working a complex button or decorative flat knot, but what looks like disaster will eventually find its final shape, and will be all the more miraculous when it is complete. Bent-nose pliers are the best tool for quickly working sections of tight, small, or complex knots, such as buttons and solid sinnets.

Learn on your own.

After you've made all the knots in this book and you're out there learning knots on your own, know that sometimes the "proper" way to tie a knot won't become clear until you've made it several times. When approaching a new knot, it's OK to just follow the knot's (hopefully clear) diagram, placing each section of cord where it is supposed to be. Learn the "what," and eventually the "how" will dawn on you. I learned countless knots this way from user-unfriendly resources. It may feel awkward, but eventually, the quick and natural way of making the knot will reveal itself. That's when the doors of creativity open.

The beauty of knotting is you can start with very little. Don't worry about running out to purchase a lot of equipment. Start with what you have; acquire materials as you need them.

ROPE & CORD

There are so many types of rope and cord with which one can knot. Generally speaking, rope comes in two structures: braid and twist (multistrand). For most purposes, I prefer cotton braid. Cotton is soft, malleable, and inexpensive, and the braid structure ensures its surface is smooth relative to the "barber pole" effect of twisted rope. For me, twisted rope's busy lines distract from the lines of the knots themselves. And twist tends to unravel, so you have to laboriously tape or whip its ends before working with it. I'll generally only use twist when a certain knot requires it, e.g., splices. If the knot doesn't require twist, I will always use braid.

When learning knots, the thicker the cord, the better. Rope with ample diameter allows you to see what you're doing, which is why kitchen twine or knitting yarn isn't best for beginners.

During the Year of Knots (as well as for the knot tutorials in this book), I used **cotton braid** in 5/16" (7.5 mm) and ¼" (6 mm) diameters almost exclusively, with the occasional 1"- (2.5 cm-) diameter **three-strand cotton** for splices.

Paracord is a thin, strong, weatherproof nylon cord originally used in parachutes. Often seen outdoors in the hands of survival gear enthusiasts, paracord comes in a rainbow of colors. Great for sinnets and knots involving multiple strands. Perfect for dog leashes.

Polypropylene, **polyester**, and **nylon** are waterproof synthetics. Be careful when purchasing polypropylene; avoid the stiff and unyielding versions. "Solid braid" polypropylene has the right amount of malleability to work for knotting, and I appreciate its soft, licorice glow that reflects light.

Manila is the classic natural fiber. It can be brutal on the hands, but when you need that rustic look, there's nothing better. Oh wait, did I say there's nothing better? In some cases, **pro-manila** will do the trick. It is a synthetic made to look and feel like classic manila, but has the added benefits of not shrinking nor rotting when wet.

Wool has a lovely, luxe hand. Wool roving is too soft and delicate to show off most knot shapes, unless that's the look you're going for, but works well when wrapped around a stiffer core. Felted wool rope is excellent for knotting.

Sailing line, arborist rope, and the like are built for hard work. Weatherproof and often light enough to float, they come in bright colors and variegated patterns.

Small stuff is technically the term for rope less than 1" in diameter, but that's by ye olde fashioned sailors' standards. I almost always use rope less than 1", so for me, materials such as **embroidery thread**, **leather lace**, and thin **satin cord** are the "small stuff."

FAVORITE
MATERIALS

Left to right

PRO-MANILA

POLYPROPYLENE SOLID BRAID

THREE-STRAND NYLON

POLYPROPYLENE BRAID

COTTON BRAID

LOVE FEST FIBERS'
"TOUGH LOVE" FELTED WOOL

WOOL WITH ROPE CORE

THREE-STRAND COTTON

COTTON BRAID

PRO-MANILA

MANILA

THREE-STRAND COTTON

NYLON BRAID

SPUN POLYPROPYLENE TWIST

FAVORITE TOOLS

There is nothing worse than a dull blade. I tie a cute Diamond Knot Tassel (page 76) to the handles of my sharp **fabric shears and scissors** to remind me they are only ever used to cut soft fiber ropes.

Craftsman Handi-Cut utility cutters slice through even 1" (2.5-cm) manila like butter. Use these when it's clear that a tough rope will ruin your shears.

Bent-nose pliers function like an extension of your hand to grip strands. After shears, the pliers are my most-reached-for tool.

Fids are tapered cylindrical tools—usually of metal, bone, or wood—that open the tight twists of multi-strand rope. Hollow fids can simultaneously hold strands open and allow splicing strands to slide through. Paracord can be stuck into the hollow rear ends of thin fids; then the fid can lead the paracord through a tightly woven piece, like a needle. With that said, don't buy a fid until you have a use for it. If all you need is to part the strands of soft, relatively thin twisted rope for splicing, a pencil or a chopstick will do. You'll know when you need a real fid.

None of the knots in this book require **corkboard** and **pins**, but those will be useful when you graduate to complex tabletop buttons and flat knots with many over-under crossings.

In the past, a sailor would use "small stuff" to whip, or wrap, the ends of thick rope to prevent its strands from unraveling. These days, it's much easier to use **tape**. I'll use **paper painters' tape** (the blue stuff) for temporary binding and **electrical tape** for a more permanent hold. When tying buttons, a **rubber band** will hold the legs together.

Most of the knots in this book are made in your hand or on the tabletop, but some projects, such as the Helix Light and the Square Knot Dog Leash (pages 44 and 50), and larger series of knots, such as nets and macramé wall pieces, will benefit from hanging. You can start making large pieces by draping your work over a door. **Hooks** on a **garment rack** are inexpensive and portable. In my studio, I've installed a wall-mounted rail on pulleys.

FAVORITE "SMALL STUFF"

Left to right

NYLON SATIN CORD (NAVY AND WHITE)

DEERSKIN LEATHER LACE (TAN AND CHOCOLATE)

24K GOLD VINTAGE JAPANESE THREAD

Left to right

DEERSKIN LEATHER LACE

NYLON SATIN CORD

PARACORD

The Tiniest Button

Turk's Head Button

Single-Strand Pretzel Button

single-strand button knots

My favorite knots to tie are buttons, a huge family of knots. At first, buttons both intimidated and fascinated me, but soon they became a recurring pleasure I revisited dozens of times during the course of the Year of Knots, making one-, two-, and even eight-strand versions.

In a completed button knot, the ends enter and exit the knot in the same place, like stems, atop which the button sits like a flower.

Button knots can be made from a single cord with a minimum of crossings, or they can be fiendishly complex. I made one that required more than thirty-five crossings and looked like disaster, until the final moments when it all came together. Buttons can comprise single cords doubled or tripled, even quadrupled, so it looks as if multiple lines run parallel through the knot, or they can be multistrand, where two or more lines chart their own *distinct* paths through the knot.

Weirdly, I rarely see these exceedingly pleasurable knots in contemporary technical knotting books, even though they are functional. Perhaps it's because, outside of traditional Chinese pajamas, we rarely use knots as actual buttons anymore. Regardless, throughout this book, I'll teach you some of my favorite varieties, starting with several easy Single-Strand Buttons and culminating in the epic Star Knot.

MATERIALS

With these beginner buttons, the thicker the rope, the better, so you can see what you're doing and thus come to understand the knot's structure.

For all of the following three buttons, I'm using ⁵⁄₁₆" (7.5 mm) cotton braid. I think ½" (2.5 cm) would be even better, as these knots compact into tiny objects. If using larger than ⁵⁄₁₆" (7.5 mm), slightly increase the recommended lengths accordingly.

KNOTS

TINIEST BUTTON

TURK'S HEAD BUTTON

SINGLE-STRAND PRETZEL BUTTON

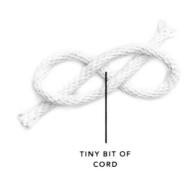

TINY BIT OF
CORD

TINIEST BUTTON

1 With 12 to 18" (30.5 to 46 cm) of cord, form a loose Overhand Knot.

Not sure what an Overhand Knot is? It is one of the most basic building-block knots. You know it already: Its shape is the first step in tying your shoes.

Notice how the Overhand Knot resembles a heart.

2 Hold down the right side of the heart, then flip the upper *left* side of the heart toward you. The knot will now look like a figure 8.

Notice the center of the knot, where a tiny bit of cord is showing through.

3 Grasp the tiny bit of cord in the center of the knot with one hand and the rope ends with the other hand. Gently pull in opposite directions.

4 Work the slack out of the "nose" so it doesn't stick up like Pinocchio's, but instead nests cutely between the two rim parts.

Work the knot snug. It should feel pillowy and soft, but have enough tension to hold itself together.

You've made your first button. Congratulations!

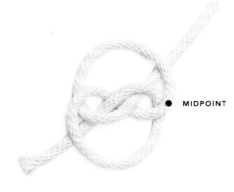

MIDPOINT

MIDPOINT

TURK'S HEAD BUTTON

1   Find the midpoint of 2′ (61 cm) of cord.

    Just to the left of the rope's midpoint, tie an Overhand Knot.

2   With the remaining right half of the rope, form a second Overhand Knot above and entwined with the first.

    Pay close attention to the over-under crossings to ensure the knot looks like the photo.

3   Gently work out the excess rope. It's easiest to do this from the center outward toward both ends.

4   Bring the two legs together, like a stem.

    The center crown should sit a little higher than the rim parts.

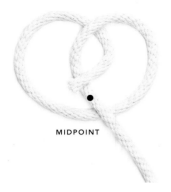

MIDPOINT

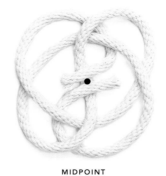

MIDPOINT

MIDPOINT
BURIED
UNDER HERE

SINGLE-STRAND PRETZEL BUTTON

Here, I'm using 3' (91 cm) of ⁵⁄₁₆"
(7.5-mm) cord.

1   Find the midpoint and arrange
    half into a pretzel shape as
    shown in the photo. Pay close
    attention to the crossings.

2   Arrange the remaining half of
    the cord into another pretzel
    entwined with the first. If you're
    a bit confused, you're not
    alone. I remember how I felt
    the first time I made this. That
    said, emulating the photo is the
    best way to learn this knot.

    Again, pay close attention to
    the crossings. It must look like
    the photo.

3   Begin to work the slack out by
    starting at the knot's center (the
    midpoint traveling under the
    two ends) and work outward
    in first one direction and then
    the other. Always work a bit of
    slack at a time, starting in the
    center of the knot, working it
    all the way to a rope end, then
    starting again at knot's center.

    The ends will get longer. Slip
    them under the rim parts.

    Note the "equals sign" in the
    center of the knot. As you're
    working the knot snug, don't let
    it get covered by the rim parts.
    Keep it above the rim. You can
    poke your finger behind it to
    prop it up.

4   Pick up the knot, letting the
    legs fall together.

    It should take but a few remain-
    ing tugs to find the knot's final,
    snug shape.

    At some point it will seem as
    if it has too many rim parts. It
    doesn't. Refer to the finished
    photo to keep nudging the rim
    parts, up and down, to find the
    final shape.

    I think this knot looks like mathe-
    matical notation! Or a letter in a
    new alphabet. I love thinking of
    the knots as language. Indeed,
    they are the language with
    which my work communicates.

practical advice for quitting a job

I found the courage to leave my job by making a money plan. The best way to create such a plan is to work with a financial adviser (which I did), but even if you can't hire an adviser—or decide not to—you can still create a detailed account of your essential expenses, how much you would need to cover them, and how much of your savings you can budget toward that goal.

I asked my financial adviser if it was insane to think about leaving, and she replied that, with a plan, nothing is insane. She reminded me that I had paid off my credit card debt a few years prior, and I had also been responsible about saving over the years for my future. So now I felt empowered to invest in my current happiness and fulfillment.

She advised me to budget a living wage by looking at my monthly expenses and deducting things I would no longer need, like gas and car expenses (no more two-hour commute), eating out every day, etc. The reality is, when you have a career you're no longer in love with, you end up spending money on little treats or diversions to get through the day. The online shopping for stuff you don't need. The wine after work to unwind. It all adds up. My advice to you is to account for that mad money and get down to the essentials you need to live (basically, housing and food), then pay yourself that amount each month out of your savings.

You could think of this plan as similar to my experience after selling the record shop, when the new owners paid me in increments over the course of a year—only you would be paying yourself. This works even if your savings account is fairly slim, and it is a realistic way to look at how much time you can dedicate to finding a new direction. It's important to have a safety net, but it doesn't have to be huge.

By making a plan, I was giving myself time to explore, because I didn't know if I'd ever make money from my creativity. The truth is, I didn't have any role models who were making a living in San Francisco solely from their art. Most supplemented with teaching or day jobs they didn't love, or had moved away from this expensive city.

Additionally—and this is key—it's important to decide how many months you want or can afford to cover to go on the journey without the pressure to immediately earn money from your creative effort. You decide how many months. The genius to this method is you make the decision once during your entire exploratory phase, rather than every month. During a period of transition, you don't want to have to repeatedly ask yourself whether it is all "worth it" or "leading somewhere." You especially don't want to have to ask yourself that at the end of each month when you're paying your bills. Transitions take time. So make the decision once . . . and don't agonize over it again. That way, you're free to listen to the voices inside of you telling you what you want to do for the rest of your life.

With my plan in place, I set out on the challenge to make my creativity my career.

rope candy

I learned the Multiple Figure 8 Knot in January 2016, the dawn of the Year of Knots. I didn't yet understand any of the jargon that I now use to describe it— racking turns, stopper knot, etc.—I just knew it seemed both useful and pretty. (And that it looked like an old-school wrapped hard candy!)

The Multiple Figure 8 is a type of stopper knot, tied at the terminal ends of rope lines in order to keep them from slipping out of a grommet or other small passage. It works brilliantly at the ends of your hoodie strings.

I play up the candy wrapper look by adding Common Whipping to the ends using "small stuff" (see Knots & Bolts, page 16).

MATERIALS

2' (61 cm) of Love Fest Fibers' "Tough Love" felted wool rope

Two 10" (25-cm) strands of 2-mm satin cord

KNOTS

MULTIPLE FIGURE 8 KNOT

COMMON WHIPPING

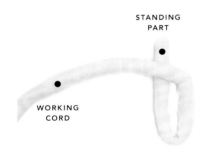

STANDING
PART

WORKING
CORD

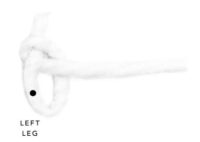

LEFT
LEG

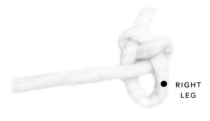

RIGHT
LEG

1 Form a skinny 3" (7.5-cm) loop at one end of the 2' (61-cm) cord, with the long working cord crossing in front of the short standing part. (The standing part of a cord is the piece that isn't actively being used at that moment. It's just standing there.)

2 Pull the working cord around behind the standing part, aka the left leg, and then forward through the loop.

3 Next, draw the working cord around and behind the right leg, then forward through the hole. Notice that, by making turns around both legs, you've made one figure 8 shape.

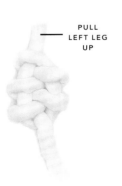

PULL
LEFT LEG
UP

LEAVE THE BIGHT
END AND THE CORD
END UNCOVERED

4 Repeat the figure 8 shape two or three more times, moving down in the loop as you go. Don't pull the turns too tight. You want the body of the knot to feel pillowy. Pull the left leg (standing part) upward to bring the figure 8s snugly together. The core cords (the legs) shouldn't be visible between the figure 8s.

5 The Common Whipping is the same knot I use to finish the ends of the Helix Light and the Star Knot (page 160). There are no bounds to the usefulness of this whipping! With one end of the satin cord, form a short bight (a curve that does not cross over itself to make a loop) and hold it against the knot with your thumb.

6 Still holding the bight with your left thumb, turn the working end compactly around the "candy wrapper" at least five times, laying the turns neatly alongside each other. Make sure to leave the end of the bight and standing end of the satin cord uncovered.

7 Thread the working end of the satin cord through the loop at the bight's end.

8 Pull the short standing end of the satin cord to the right, which draws the tiny bight loop under the turns. You should feel a satisfying *plunk* as it pops under the turns. Don't pull too far; keep it buried under the turns. Trim both ends of the satin cord.

PULL STANDING END RIGHT

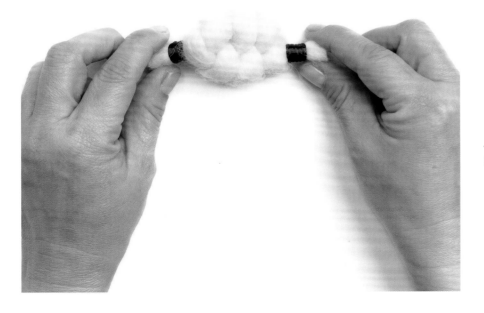

9 Repeat the Common Whipping on the other side of the "candy." Trim excess rope so just a bit remains. Fluff/fray the rope ends of the "candy wrapper."

multiple figure 8+ necklace and the corkscrew

Soon after learning the Multiple Figure 8 Knot, which I christened Rope Candy (page 26), I became curious about the creative possibilities inherent in extending these wrapped, sliding-core, noose-like structures.

In order to fill the longer outside curves in the pieces I had in mind, it seemed logical to add extra turns on one of the legs of the Multiple Figure 8. Has this structure been documented and named yet, I wonder? For now, I'm calling it the Multiple Figure 8+ Knot.

Happily, the experiments proved successful and produced the Multiple Figure 8+ Necklace and its logical extension, the Corkscrew.

MATERIALS

15' (4.6 m) of ¼" (6-mm) cotton braid for the Multiple Figure 8+ Necklace

30' (9.1 m) of ¼" (6-mm) cotton braid for The Corkscrew

← 4' (1.2 M)

BEGIN
KNOTTING
HERE

← 11' (3.4 M)

LONG
WORKING
CORD

THE MULTIPLE FIGURE 8+ NECKLACE

If this is your first time tying this knot, I suggest making it on a tabletop.

1 Start with the 15' (4.6 m) of rope. Divide it into two parts at the 4' (1.2-m) point.

At the 4' (1.2-m) point, double the 11' (3.4-m) part of the rope back about 1' (30.5 cm), forming a skinny horizontal loop, and begin knotting here. The lower 11' (3.4-m) length is the working cord.

With the working cord, wrap one tight turn around the standing upper leg of the loop, ending by drawing the working cord back to front through the loop.

2 Hold the first turn tight against the tabletop with your left fingers, then wrap *two* turns around the lower leg, again ending by drawing the working cord back to front through the loop hole. Note that this is the figure 8 shape with an extra turn on the lower leg.

Tip: With line this long, it's easier to form the turns not by grabbing the line's end, but by working with the part of the line that's already at the point where the turns will live. Make the turns, then pull the long working end through the loop back to front.

3 Continue these same three turns working toward the right, always alternating between one turn on the upper leg, then two turns on the lower leg.

Make *tight* turns, not loose ones.

Tip: To keep the knot in place, always use your fingers to hold down the last couple of turns.

LAST TWO TURNS
ARE ON
LOWER LEG

4 Count the turns on the upper leg. You want about twelve turns (this will vary according to the thickness of rope you're using).

Make sure the last two turns are on the *lower* leg.

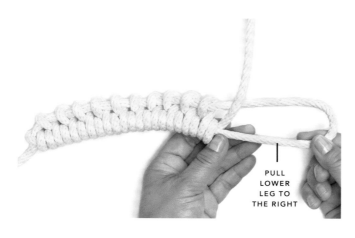

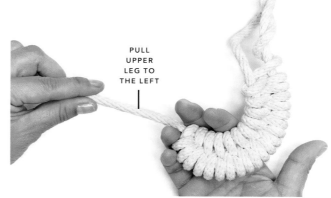

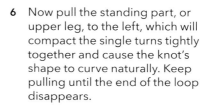

5 Pull the lower leg firmly to the right, compacting the double turns quite tightly.

It's important to do this step. If you forget, the knot will feel loose and won't retain its shape.

6 Now pull the standing part, or upper leg, to the left, which will compact the single turns tightly together and cause the knot's shape to curve naturally. Keep pulling until the end of the loop disappears.

7 If the number of single turns was correctly proportional to the width of the cord used, you will have a lovely semicircle.

The ends of the necklace may be secured with any number of knots; I suggest the Triple English Knot (page 84), which allows the necklace's length to be adjusted.

Cute, right?

THE CORKSCREW

The success with the Multiple Figure 8+ Knot warranted even further investigation.

It seemed as if the curve would, given enough length, spiral back on itself. Happily, my guess was correct.

Here, I've made the knot with 30' (9.1 m) of ¼" (6-mm) rope and only stopped making the turns when I ran out of rope. I ended up with at least fifty single turns on the upper leg.

When the upper leg is pulled left quite tightly, this ruffled rope creature emerges.

When its ruffles are smoothed into neat curves with your fingers, the rope creature resolves itself into this deliciously perfect spiral.

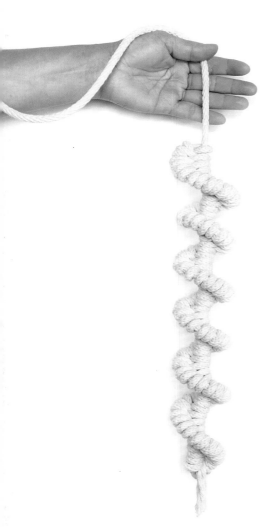

the path

During the first few weeks after I left my job, I thought hard about the next steps. I knew I wanted to work with my hands, but what form would my creativity take? I had many ideas of tactile things I could do and make. Would I seek a degree? The range of possibilities was immense . . . but not paralyzing. I've always been voracious about new experiences, and I was ravenous. If you're ravenous, too, great! *You* are who I wrote this book for. Learning knots is a wonderful way to get your hands moving, and once they're moving, eventually you will find your own medium and your own style will begin to emerge.

I left no stone unturned. I embarked on a self-directed program of classes in every topic I was even slightly interested in: wood turning, ceramics, block printing, natural dye, wood and stone carving, weaving, macramé, interior design, and LED wiring. When I discovered that I didn't enjoy something, I rejoiced: **Knowing what you don't like is valuable information. Even fails and dead ends have much to teach us.** For example, I tried ceramics on a weekly basis for six months, only to eventually throw up my hands and admit I hate working with messy liquids. And when I took an interior design introductory class, I soon realized it reminded me too much of my past careers of curating other people's work.

The only two forms that stuck with me were wood carving and macramé. So I dove deep into both. Wooden spoon carving led to spoon sales and then a newfound passion as a popular spoon carving teacher. Standard macramé beginner projects such as plant hangers led to the development of the Helix Light, and then to room-size, site-specific rope installations, the work I do today.

Finding your voice sounds like a big (and possibly intimidating) deal, but the reality is that it happens in small increments and subtle shifts. Now that it's been a few years, I look back on this phase and see that I was slowly developing proficiency by learning individual skills. If you are like me, you value expertise. And you want to get past the basics to start being not just an artisan, but an artisan with a point of view and a clear aesthetic. It will happen. **Once your skills have reached a certain level, your own voice will emerge, and the work will begin to reflect who you are.** It doesn't happen immediately, and you can't rush it. In fact, I hope you'll enjoy the journey as much as I did. Learning is a wonderful phase to be in, because anything seems possible.

With the above in mind, I knew that if I wanted to make a living making products, they needed to be unique. Within the maker and art worlds, it's poor etiquette to replicate someone else's work at the expense of finding your own voice. But it's also true that on your journey, you'll probably make early work that strongly resembles, even imitates, the work of artists who inspire you. That's normal, so just keep in mind a simple principle of artistic integrity: Take care not to step on others' toes if you haven't found your unique voice yet. For

instance, with this book, I hope you will learn some knots that become personal favorites, but if your aim is to *sell* knot-based products, I invite you to evolve *your own design*. You will absolutely know when you've found your voice, and the achievement will taste all the more sweet when it is genuinely yours.

Without purposely thinking about it, I intuitively moved from making something functional to making a uniquely designed object. I knew how to carve wooden spoons, but that in and of itself wasn't interesting enough for me. So I created my own design, something I'd never seen before: a spoon with a right-angle corner element (page 56) that not only allowed the spoon to be used as a spatula, but also was conceptually pure and simple. I thought the corner design element was the perfect marriage of function and aesthetic. It embodied my values. And the spoons turned into my first big creative success.

At about this time, I was talking to a business coach who brought a phrase out of me that has become a guiding principle: **"Elevating the everyday" became my mantra.**

I think all of us—regardless of income, no matter where we are in life—have the ability to pause and regard what's right in front of us and appreciate the moment. Appreciate the everyday. Spoons are common objects, but if you're using a spoon you carved yourself, you've elevated that moment. It can be sublime. Similarly, when I see beautiful lamps suspended from sad, naked electrical cables, I see an opportunity lost. Why can't that functional piece be part of a beautiful, elevated moment as well? That's how I started making my Helix Lights.

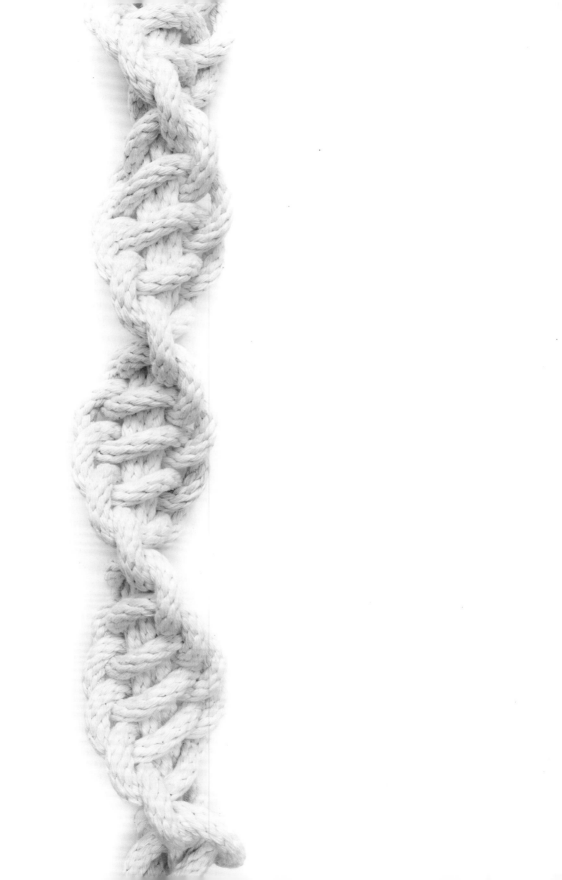

classic macramé knots: half knot and square knot

Macramé knots are a small but interesting category of the larger world of knotting, and reportedly originated with sailors making decorative work in their downtime. It enjoyed a heyday in the 1960s and '70s, and today, a new generation of makers is discovering the craft.

The classic knots used most often in macramé are the Half Knot and the Square Knot. With just these two knots and a handful of others tied in repeated patterns, infinitely varied designs can result.

It's important to learn these basic knots, but my additional hope (and the point of this book) is that you'll go beyond them. The more knots you know, the more expressive your work will be. Learn these . . . and then learn more.

The **Half Knot** is the building block knot that is the basis of so many others. What's a Half Knot? You know it already: It is the same over-under first step in tying your shoes, before you add the bow. (The Half Knot is closely related to the Overhand Knot in that they share the same shape. However, the Half Knot binds *around* an object while the Overhand does not; the latter is primarily pulled tight to use as a *stopper* knot.)

When multiple, identical Half Knots are repeatedly tied in a vertical stack around a core, they will naturally spiral into the **Twisted Bar**. Known by many other names—Half Knot Spiral, Bannister Bar, Half Square Knot Spiral— this element comprises either all left Half Knots or all right Half Knots. We don't care whether the Half Knots are tied to the left or right, only that they are consistently *all* left or *all* right.

On the other hand, a left Half Knot stacked atop a right Half Knot (or vice versa) results in the classic **Square Knot** (or Reef Knot), and when *this* sequence is stacked repeatedly around a core, the **Solomon Bar** results.

MATERIALS

Both the Twisted Bar and the Solomon Bar can be made with practically any type and width of cord. I've even made them with Ethernet cable.

KNOTS

HALF KNOT

SQUARE KNOT

TWISTED BAR

SOLOMON BAR

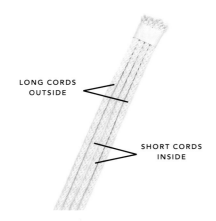

LONG CORDS OUTSIDE

SHORT CORDS INSIDE

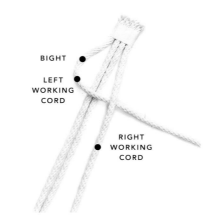

BIGHT

LEFT WORKING CORD

RIGHT WORKING CORD

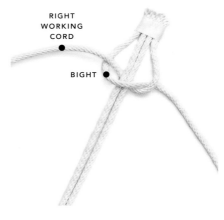

RIGHT WORKING CORD

BIGHT

In macramé, the core is often simply two filler cords, which are there to provide sufficient width to form an attractive bar.

1   Measure out four cords in a material of your choice. In this tutorial, I'm using a pair of 1′ (30.5-cm) filler cords and a pair of 4′ (1.2-m) working cords, all out of ¼″ (6-mm) cotton braid. The length of the fillers represents what the length of the finished bars will be. The pair of outer working cords should be four or five times the length of the filler cords.

2   Both the Twisted Bar and the Solomon Bar begin with the same first **Half Knot**.

    To make the Half Knot, arrange the cords so that the longer ones are on the right and left, framing the pair of short filler cords in the center.

3   Bind the ends together. Here, I've taped them to a tabletop for simplicity, but for a longer bar, you can secure them with a rubber band or Constrictor Knot (page 78) and hang from a hook or rail.

4   To tie a Half Knot around the filler cords, draw the left working cord across the front of the fillers and *behind* the right working cord.

    Notice the open curve (or bight) formed by the left working cord.

5   Next, draw the right working cord leftward behind the crossed cord and the filler cords and pull forward through the bight.

    Gently pull the working cords outward to draw the knot snug.

    This is your Half Knot. From here, we can make the Twisted Bar or the Solomon Bar.

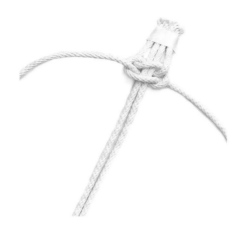  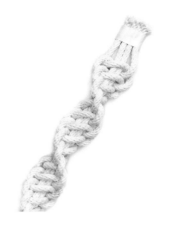

THE TWISTED BAR

1 Continue forming identical Half Knots, always starting by *first* moving the left cord toward the right.

The photo shows two identical Half Knots, stacked.

As you continue knotting, you can see how the Twisted Bar gets its name. Isn't it beautiful?

2 At some point, about every six or seven knots, the "front" of the bar will seem to have spiraled so far to the right that you notice your body going with it. Don't let this happen: Ergonomics are so important when you knot in quantity. Take care of your body!

As soon as you feel yourself leaning right with the bar, simply let go of the working cords and center yourself in front of the bar again. What used to be the back of the bar, now regard as the front (lean left a little).

The working cord that was dropped from your right hand is picked up by your left hand, and vice versa. Continue knotting exactly as before (even though it feels like you're facing the "back" of the bar), and you'll be happily surprised to see that the knot continues to spiral.

3 Whether you like a tight or a relaxed look, it's important to be consistent. I get a lot of satisfaction out of each knot's finishing "tug." For a tidy Twisted Bar, apply to each tug the same amount of pressure each time.

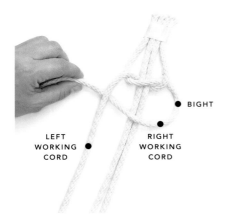

LEFT
WORKING
CORD

RIGHT
WORKING
CORD

BIGHT

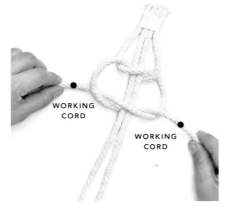

WORKING
CORD

WORKING
CORD

THE SQUARE KNOT AND THE SOLOMON BAR

1 To make a Square Knot, start with a Half Knot (page 38), then begin alternating which cord moves first.

Since we made our first Half Knot by moving the *left* working cord first, the second Half Knot is formed by moving the right working cord first. Draw it leftward in front of the filler cords and behind the left working cord.

Notice the bight formed on the right.

2 Now draw the left working cord to the right, going *behind* the crossed right cord and the fillers and forward through the bight.

Notice that the working cords have changed position. To avoid confusion, just think of them as "working cords," period.

3 Draw the knot up snugly. This is a Square Knot.

4 To make the Solomon Bar, continue making Square Knots. In other words, continue making Half Knots—starting with the left cord again—and then keep alternating which cord moves first.

Unlike the Twisted Bar, the Solomon Bar stays flat, like a ribbon. Properly made, this elegant structure has a pleasing bulk relative to the size of the cords used to make it. It feels good in the hand, which is why I think it's perfect as a dog leash (page 50).

helix light

Less than a year into my creative journey, I noticed a theme common to all the objects I felt compelled to make: They elevate the everyday. I love creating opportunities to appreciate ordinary moments and quotidian items. Just as a hand-carved wood spoon elevates my morning coffee and a knotted pendant light brightens my home, I believe this attitude toward appreciating handmade objects can improve anyone's quality of life. As the essayist Rebecca Solnit points out:

"[I]t's the job of artists to find out how materials and images speak, to make the mute material world come to life. . . . Words of gold, of paint, of velvet, of steel, the speaking shapes and signs that we learn to read, the intelligence of objects set free . . . to teach us that all things communicate, that a spoon has something to say about values, as does a shoe rack or a nice ornamental border of tulips or freesias."*

The Helix Light is an example of marrying such artistic passion with practicality by turning a simple knot into a beautiful household item.

MATERIALS

Two 80' (24.4-m) strands of ¼" (6-mm) cotton braid

Several rubber bands

One 17' (5.2-m) strand of ¼" (6-mm) cotton braid

One 15' (4.6-m) pendant light with built-in socket, switch, and plug (such as the ready-made ones from the ColorCord Company; see Resources, page 190)

Electrical tape (optional)

Two 2' (61-cm) strands of ¼" (6-mm) cotton braid

(don't cut these now; you may be able to use the trimmed excess from the 80'/24.4-m lengths)

Lightbulb (I like oversize 5"/13-cm globe bulbs, the G40 size with a standard E26 base)

If you're making a lamp of a length other than 15' (4.6 m), or covering another type of thin cable, the rule of thumb for ¼" (6-mm) rope is to use at least five times the length of the final piece.

KNOTS

TWISTED BAR
 (page 41)

COMMON WHIPPING
 (page 28)

*Excerpt copyright © Rebecca Solnit, first printed in *The Encylopedia of Trouble And Spaciousness* (Trinity University Press, Nov. 2014).

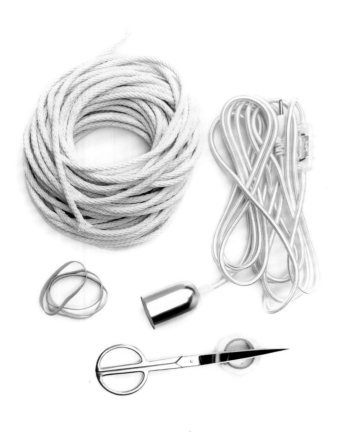

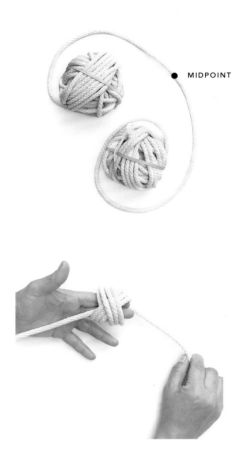

MIDPOINT

Eighty feet of rope is a huge amount! Make it easy on yourself by knotting the light as two long halves. The idea is to start knotting at the light cable's midpoint and work to the end, then return to the halfway point and work toward the other end. Otherwise, you're having to schlep eighty-foot basketballs of rope with each knot you tie. Don't do that. When you knot, take care of your body.

To prepare, find the midpoint of each of the long 80′ (24.4-m) ropes. Make two balls on each cord, as shown in the photo. Wind tight, compact balls around your fingers, like yarn balls, starting a couple of feet from the midpoint and working toward the end, finishing with the end of the rope on the outside of the ball.

Secure each ball with two or more strong rubber bands, doubling the bands if necessary so they're secure. As you knot, the rope is drawn from the inside of the ball.

Some fiber artists suggest making "tamales" instead of balls by winding the rope in a figure 8 pattern around the thumb and pinkie, but I find it too difficult to make tamales with large amounts of thick rope.

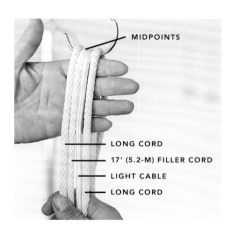

MIDPOINTS

LONG CORD
17' (5.2-M) FILLER CORD
LIGHT CABLE
LONG CORD

1 Find the midpoint of each of the two 80' (24.4-m) cords, the 17' (5.2-m) cord, and the light cable.

Tightly secure all four midpoints together with a rubber band or, if you're a badass, a firm Constrictor Knot (page 78). You don't want any of the midpoints to shift. If preventing that becomes a problem, you can tie all four into a giant Overhand Knot (page 122) at the midpoint. Keep the half of everything that you're not knotting out of the way.

I use hooks to hang the whole setup from a rolling garment rack. If you're not ready to invest in that, draping over a door, shower rod, or cup hook works, or you can jerry-rig something equally simple.

2 Arrange the four cords so the long ones are on the outside and the filler cord and light cable are inside.

3 Grasp the long cords in your right and left hands, and begin making the Twisted Bar (page 41) around the filler cords, i.e., the 17' (5.2-m) piece and the light cable.

You will have to pull a rope ball through the bight each time. This may seem like a pain, but it's faster than pulling forty feet of loose rope. You'll get the hang of it quickly. I actually enjoy the rhythmic flow of tossing the bundled balls.

4 When you need more length in the working cords, gently pull on the rope ball to release some length from its center. When necessary, tighten the rubber bands and/or re-wind the ball so rope does not slip out unintentionally.

Remember, when the front face of the Twisted Bar spirals so far to the right that you find yourself leaning toward it, you don't have to follow that face. Simply release the knotting, move your hands to the left, and pick up opposite cords on the back face, knotting exactly the same way that you did on the front face.

When you approach one of the ends of the light cable, either the plug or socket, stop knotting about two inches from above the plug or socket.

Return to the midpoint of the lamp and continue the Twisted Bar toward the other end.

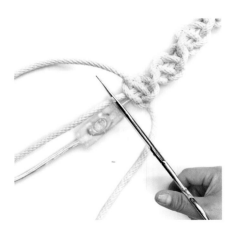  

HOW TO
HANDLE THE LIGHT SWITCH

5 About an inch from the light switch (typically located 2'/61 cm from the plug), cut the filler cord and save it to add back in below the switch. Continue knotting with the outer working cords until you are flush against the switch.

6 Pull the outer working cords down tight against both sides of the switch, framing it. Rope, being made of fiber, will inevitably loosen over time, so it's best to get it as tight as possible now.

Hold one end of the saved filler cord against the light cable below the switch and continue knotting around it and the light cable, working your way down to the plug.

HOW TO
FINISH THE ENDS

7 To give the Twisted Bar a polished finish, the method is the same for both the plug and the socket ends of the light: apply a **Common Whipping** (page 28). If you've already learned Rope Candy (page 26), you know the Common Whipping.

This is one of the most gloriously useful, tidy knots. Traditionally applied to thick rope ends to prevent fraying, it comes in handy anytime I need to seize, or bind, cords together, such as the stem of the Star Knot (page 160).

Trim the three ends of the Twisted Bar cords, leaving 2" (5 cm) intact.

Tightly tape the three ends to the light cable using electrical tape. This is optional, but I like to do it.

8 Using one of your 2' (61-cm) rope lengths (which may have come from the excess material trimmed off the working cords) form a 3" (7.5-cm), narrow, U-shaped loop and hold it against the taped cord/cable bundle. The loop end should overlap the plug, and the standing end should overlap onto the Twisted Bar.

9 With the working end, make snug coils (turns) around the loop and cord bundle, taking care to keep the coils uniform and leaving the loop and standing end exposed.

10 After at least four coils, insert the working end through the small loop.

Adjust the tightness of the coils to ensure they're neither too tight nor too loose. They should be of uniform size.

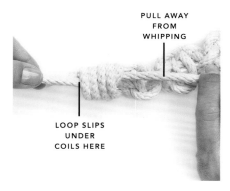

Look at that clean finish!

11 Holding the working end with your left hand, pull the standing end away from the whipping with your right, which will cause the loop to slip under the coils, hiding it.

12 Trim both ends.

square knot dog leash

I don't know about your dog, but given the chance, my greyhound, Shelley Duvall, will chase a motorcycle down the street. For her, I need a strong leash. There are all sorts of rope leashes I could have whipped up, but my main concern was that I wanted to be free from worrying the leash would fail. Therefore, I challenged myself to design a leash that met the following requirements:

[1] It would be made from just a single length of cord, cutting down to zero the number of connecting knots that might possibly break apart (not that *my* knots would ever fail, but you know what I mean!), and

[2] The ends would be incorporated into the handle in such a way that the dog pulling on the leash would not put strain on them.

I specifically chose to use the classic Square Knot Solomon Bar for its bulk (I hate skinny leashes) and because it feels good in the hand.

MATERIALS

80' (24.4-m) of ¼" (6-mm) polypropylene solid braid (makes a 5'/1.5-m leash)

Metal split-ring key ring or swivel snap hook

Rubber bands (optional)

Bent-nose pliers

KNOTS

SOLOMON BAR
(page 42)

To stay consistent with the rest of this book, I'm demonstrating the dog leash using white cotton braid, but for maximum functionality, the leash should be made from weatherproof rope.

Choose a cord width that is proportional to the size of your dog. For my full-size greyhound, ¼" (6 mm) is fine, but it is weighty. You don't want to drag the dog down. For smaller dogs, or if you just like a lighter leash, paracord would be perfect, and there are beautiful vintage and new polypropylene ropes that are practically weightless.

Shelley Duvall, my greyhound

Clogs by Bryr
Jumpsuit by Ilana Kohn

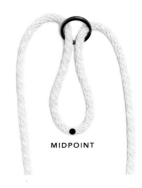

MIDPOINT

---

1   Fold the rope in half at its midpoint.

Insert the midpoint back to front through the key ring or swivel snap hook, forming a loop.

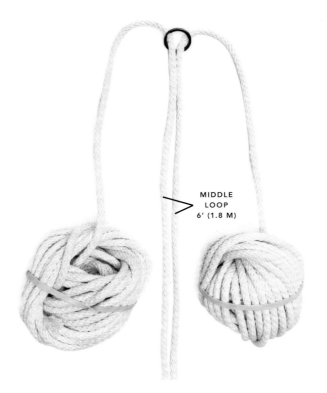

MIDDLE
LOOP
6' (1.8 M)

---

2   Pull the loop through the key ring for a length of 6' (1.8 m). Five feet of this long loop will become the leash; the sixth foot will become the handle.

If desired, bundle the long ends tightly into rope balls (see page 46) and secure with at least one rubber band (or more). Or, you can leave the ropes loose and unbundled for a great arm workout.

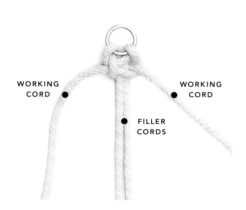  

WORKING CORD

WORKING CORD

FILLER CORDS

3 The only knot required is the Square Knot Solomon Bar (page 41), which you will recall is one right Half Knot and one left Half Knot stacked atop each other. The two legs of the long center loop act as the filler cords.

Make the first Square Knot around the filler cords. Make sure the knot is snug against the key ring or swivel snap hook.

4 Continue making the Solomon Bar.

Take special care to ensure the knots are tightly packed against each other. You can physically push them upward with your hand. If they're not densely stacked when the leash stretches, the knots will stretch apart, too, and things will look sloppy. You want a firm, elegant leash that does not distort.

5 When the Solomon Bar is 5' (1.5 m) long, with only 1' (30.5 cm) of filler cord remaining, stop knotting.

Flip the bottom of the loop upward, forming two lobes.

6 Bring the two lobes together by tucking the right lobe behind the left. The loop should be crossing over itself, forming a double loop.

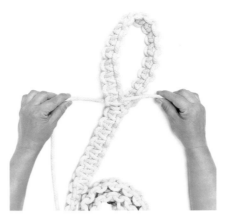

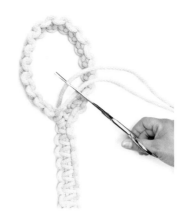

KNOT DOWN
THIS SIDE OF
THE LOOP

7 Now here's the key:

Don't continue to knot following the filler cords to the right. Instead, knot down the *left* side of the double loop.

By doing this, you're ensuring the loop will be bound to itself, virtually unbreakable and very secure.

8 Keep knotting all the way around the loop.

9 When you've knotted over the entirety of the loop/handle, trim the ends to 3" (7.5 cm).

Notice the side of the handle that you've just finished knotting. You will tuck the trimmed ends up the *other* side of the handle, in effect continuing to circle the handle.

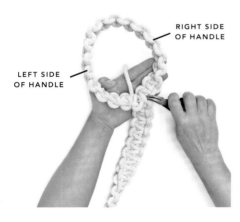

LEFT SIDE
OF HANDLE

RIGHT SIDE
OF HANDLE

10 To repeat: In this photo, we just finished knotting the left side of the handle; therefore, we will tuck the trimmed ends up the *right* side of the handle.

Tuck the ends into the insides of the Square Knots as if the ends were extra filler cord. Tuck them at least three or four "stitches" deep apiece. The bent-nose pliers come in handy here to grasp the ends for pulling through.

When the cords are fully tucked, trim any excess.

If you're using paracord or another synthetic, you can carefully melt the ends with a lighter to prevent unraveling.

The leash that won't fail.

immersion
in craft and
products

As I began my year of living creatively, I threw myself into making functional (and beautiful) products to sell. It seemed practical, and I had observed people doing that and making a living. Of course, the maker movement was in full swing. Wooden spoons were definitely a thing in 2016, as were hand-thrown pots, small-batch jewelry, all-natural bath products, and the like. **Anyone can be a maker, but for me, the best work speaks simply and elegantly.**

I encourage you to raise your own awareness about what draws you most powerfully. This is a clue to your next move. For me, it was objects made by craftspeople at the top of their game, whose products were an embodiment of the makers' values. I wanted to be one of those people. When I got accepted to West Coast Craft, a carefully curated craft fair of makers, I encountered an aesthetic I respected and a selective process that felt special. I had found my tribe.

I'm very deadline-driven, and the upcoming craft fair gave me the perfect motivation to set inventory goals, establish a real online presence, name my company, and—with a friend from Apple—design a logo.

Lots of people say it's unwise to use your real name for your company, the reason being that you may one day want to sell the company; therefore, you should think long-term. But, in the world of *fine art*, artists sign their names to their work. So think about this "products versus art" distinction, and have that conversation with yourself when considering your own branding. For me, using my given name as opposed to a made-up brand felt like the right decision, and this was an early inkling that I wanted to retain authorship of my work. My work was so personal, and so tied to my values, I couldn't imagine being distanced from what I was making. It was a part of me and I wanted to treat it the way fine artists do. You might feel differently when it comes to naming your own endeavor, and that is absolutely OK. Trust your instincts above all else.

While this was my first recognition of the tension between product and art, it was the beginning of a series of subsequent revelations about the differences . . . and the inevitable shift I'd be making. I was finding success and interest in my work, but just as quickly, it was dawning on me that a business dependent on making products means tackling challenges like volume, scale, packaging, cost-efficient production, fulfillment, product consistency, and repetition (and its inevitable by-product:

boredom). Not to mention the threat of copycat "handcrafted" products mass-produced by so many trendy mall retailers. I could see that I might spend all this time scaling my business to a certain level only to be knocked off once it crossed a certain threshold of visibility. Not what I had signed up for.

Additionally, I realized that once I had perfected the Helix Light, *making* it didn't feel as creative as when I was developing and refining its design. The process had moved from creation to production. (Indeed, today, after having made many hundreds of Helix Lights, the joy I get from them has shifted from the making to personally installing multiples of them in my clients' spaces, where finding fresh ways to drape them in a chandelier array is what feels new each time.) In other words, I had just begun to dive into this business, and already I could sense that products alone would not keep me creatively engaged.

That aside, as a blossoming entrepreneur, I was doing well for myself. It was a fun challenge to figure out how to make the business viable. I tackled production issues and the wholesale-versus-retail debate with enthusiasm, at least at first. If you've begun selling your work, then you know that pricing is among the most interesting challenges you will run across. For example, when I looked at what other craftspeople on Etsy were charging, I could easily tell who was a hobbyist and who was making a living. When I saw someone selling their handmade object for, say, $25, and I knew it probably took two hours to make, I could see that, had the maker considered the equation, they valued their time at $12.50/hour—not to mention the work it took to design and develop the piece, plus materials costs and more. I had higher ambitions than $12.50 an hour—and you should, too. Know that your work has inherently

more value than the time it took to make . . . because *you* made it. My thought is this: My work is valuable because I bring to it a deep understanding of the form, the materials, and the work's context in craft history, and, most importantly, my own aesthetic. The reason someone would choose my product over a lower-priced piece is because they value everything I bring to the table.

I encourage you to look honestly at your work and assess not only time and materials, but your expertise, aesthetic, and experience. I encourage you to value your time and your unique point of view. This should help you arrive at a true reflection of the value of your work.

Don't let my personal experience of dissatisfaction with product-making dissuade you; if you have an idea for a product and discover that there is demand, it can be a great way to make a living. You can also evolve that product into new versions of itself, or expand into a line. Another way to look at this is: Choose the line of work that will present problems you *like* solving. **You can't get away from problems and challenges in life, so choose the problems you want to figure out.** For me, the dilemma is how not to get bored and how to keep evolving my work. For someone else, figuring out how to grow a retail business and solve problems of scale and volume may be genuinely exciting and energizing.

Although I had no way of knowing at the time, the problem of keeping my work interesting was the greatest gift. It led me to one of the best ideas I've ever had. Paying close attention to my feelings around being a maker of product—and everything that entailed—helped me find my truth. As soon as something ceased to be interesting, I was attuned enough to my process and my journey to know it was time to move forward.

doughnut knot

Because I learned it on the Year of Knots' very first day, the Doughnut will always be among my favorites. You may have seen it used as a window shade pull. It was invented by Clifford Ashley himself, who includes it in the *Ashley Book of Knots* chapter on single-strand terminal knots. True to their name, terminal—or stopper—knots are found most often at the ends of lines in order to prevent line from slipping out of a desired position. The Doughnut is more complicated and decorative than a stopper needs to be, but it is an undeniably fun delight to make (and a good party trick).

The knot can be made with cord thicker or thinner than what I've specified, in which case you may want to adjust the knot's desired circumference accordingly. So much of knot tying is about getting the proportions of rope size versus knot size to look "right," and it may take a few tries with various cord diameters and fibers for the aesthetics to fall into place. You will know when you've found the perfect proportions . . . and the knotter in her element will enjoy the hunt.

MATERIALS

11' (3.4 m) of ¼" (6-mm) cotton braid will make a palm-size Doughnut

STANDING END

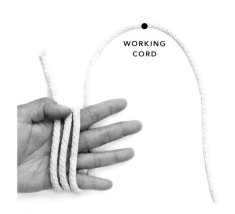

WORKING CORD

1 Hold the rope in your palm with the short end pointing up. This is the standing end of the rope.

2 Wrap the rope loosely around the palm three times, finishing with the working cord behind the palm traveling upward. You should see three sections of the rope on your palm, and, similarly, three sections of the rope on the back of your hand.

3 Remove the three loops from your hand, holding the top of the loops with your fingers. The working cord should be in front of the standing end and heading leftward.

LITTLE SCARF

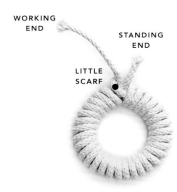

WORKING END

STANDING END

LITTLE SCARF

4 Wrap the working cord clockwise, behind and around the standing end, like a little scarf.

5 Moving clockwise, form tight little coils around the Doughnut, drawing the cord through the hole to the back each time.

   Densely pack the coils against each other. You want a firm Doughnut. To keep the coils snug and in place, always tightly hold the last coil you made.

6 When the loops are completely covered by the coils, look at the little scarf surrounding the standing end.

   Pull the working end of the rope up through the scarf, right next to the standing end and traveling in the same direction.

   Trim the ends as desired.

gift knot

Let's first get familiar with the **Carrick Bend** shape (see page 74).

Bends are the huge family of knots that unite two lines, or the two ends of a single line.

The Carrick Bend shown here is indeed uniting two cords. (Q: How do we know that at a glance? A: Because we see four ends.) The Gift Knot, on the other hand, actually unites the two ends of the single line that is wrapping around the package. Both qualify as Carricks.

A defining feature of the Carrick Bend is that each cord, in its journey through the knot, will consistently alternate under and over at the crossings. If you are ever looking at a similarly shaped knot that does not precisely alternate between under and over crossings, it is not a Carrick Bend and may be unsafe for use, liable to spill, slip, or jam.

MATERIALS

5' (1.5 m) of ⁵⁄₁₆" (7.5-mm) cotton braid *plus* **the circumference of the box**

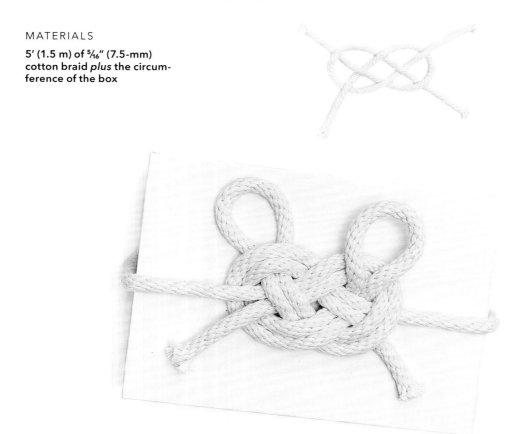

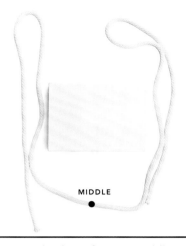

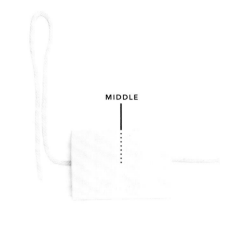

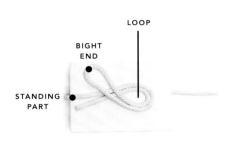

1 To make the **Gift Knot**, middle the cord.

Double the ends by folding them back on themselves on either side of the box.

2 Center the box over the cord's middle and prepare to make the left half of the bend.

3 Treat the doubled left end as a single cord. Keep it flat and untwisted, like a ribbon. Lay it over the box and lay the bight end back *over* the standing part, so the bight is pointing upward.

Notice the loop created on the right.

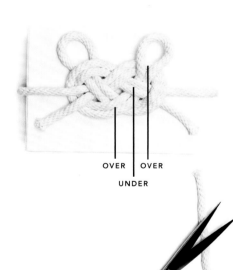

5 To finish the knot, lead the working end upward *over* the bottom part of the loop, but crossing *under* its own standing part behind the loop—then finish by pulling *over* the top half of the loop. Remember the crossing sequence is *over-under-over*.

Work out the slack, making sure it is snug around the box and the "bunny ears" are of equal size.

Trim the ends.

4 Treating the doubled right cord as a single line, lead it upward and leftward *under* the loop, continuing *over* the left bight end, and down *under* the left standing part.

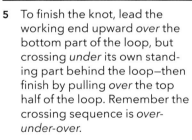

gift knot

63

start where you are

Rather than listen to external voices telling you what you should be doing, dig deeper and uncover the things that truly resonate with you, the things you love. *They are already in there*. They are not disparate; they are not random. *You* are the connection.

Sometimes, things so close to you, things *about yourself*, are painfully obvious when you see them in retrospect, though it's impossible to make the connection while something's happening in the moment. During my first year post-Apple, while I explored more than a dozen different forms of artistic expression, only woodworking and macramé instantly clicked for me. Literally within five minutes of doing each of those activities in a class, I thought, "I *love* this."

It makes all the sense in the world that the two disciplines I was drawn to were wood and rope: These were the materials my parents chose. My father was a hobbyist woodworker and my mom had taught me macramé during its hippie heyday. But it wasn't until months after I'd committed to these crafts that it occurred to me to make the connection. No wonder they resonated so deeply! Those early experiences, those familiarities with the sights and sounds, look and feel, of wood and rope had lain dormant for years, only to blossom once I dedicated myself to my own creativity. **The things that you experience as a child have deep resonance in you, even if they remain unrecognized until the time comes.**

Similarly, my love for master designer Massimo Vignelli's iconic New York City subway map was born initially because I saw it so much as a child, when visiting my grandmother in Flushing, Queens, every weekend. The map is a design triumph because it communicates, via a few simple lines and colors, all the complexity of a municipal travel system. It is a formative image that continues to deeply influence my aesthetic . . . though I could not have articulated that fact until decades later. When I finally connected the lines in my knots with Vignelli's lines, I felt breathless, in awe of the power of early experiences.

Steve Jobs delivered a relevant anecdote in his 2005 Stanford commencement speech. Once he dropped *out* of Reed College, not seeing the value in pursuing a degree, he proceeded to drop *in* on classes he was truly interested in. With curiosity and intuition guiding him, he took, of all things, a calligraphy class. There, he learned about proportionally spaced fonts and serifs. He never once expected this to have any practical application in his life, yet ten years later, it came back to him. Beautiful typography was written into the Mac's first operating system and set the standard for personal computers.

Steve summed up the lesson like this: "You can't connect the dots looking forward; you can only connect them looking backward. So you have to trust that the dots will somehow connect in your future. You have to trust in something—your gut, destiny, life, karma, whatever. This approach has never let me down, and it has made all the difference in my life."

Start wherever you are. It is never too late; it's already there inside you, waiting. Be confident that your aesthetic is your unique fingerprint, and pursue the expression of it relentlessly.

gold chain sinnet

A big part of the joy of sinnets is the repetitive nature of the making. It feels good to immerse myself in the flow of it, my fingers busy, my brain free to fly. The word *sinnet* may be related to the word *knit*, and both pursuits do share that same quality of allowing one to feel blissfully productive.

Sinnets comprise several subfamilies, including crown sinnets (page 95), flat plaits (braids), loop sinnets, solid sinnets, chain sinnets (the topic of this tutorial), and more. They can range from incredibly simple, single-line loop chains—like the "monkey chain" from childhood—to complex multistrand beasts. I once saw a video of the making of a *121-strand* solid sinnet.

As someone who went to high school in the '80s, I recall when fat gold chains from the golden age of hip-hop were an iconic look. In fact, when I made this sinnet of interlocking double rings, my first thought was the cover of the classic Eric B. and Rakim album *Paid in Full*. So I refer it to it as the bling-iest of braids: the Gold Chain Sinnet.

As you're making the sinnet, decide how loose or tight you'll want its "links" to be. In this tutorial, because the cord is so fluffy, I've kept the chain loose. For other types of cord, especially smaller or less soft ones, you may wish to create a tighter chain with smaller "links," which will be no less beautiful.

MATERIALS

Tape

20' (6.1 m) of felted yarn (such as Love Fest Fibers' "Tough Love," which is about ½"/1.3 cm wide) makes a 2'- (61-cm-) long, loose-linked sinnet.

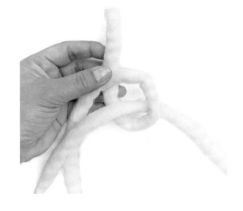

1   Apply tape to one end of the rope in a tapered, pointed shape that is thinner than the rope itself. This is the working end.

2   Hold the standing end of the cord and make a loop as shown.

The standing end is *behind* the loop.

3   Draw the working end of the cord from back to front through the loop, then pull through so it forms a second, similarly sized loop.

4   For the third pass, draw the working cord through *both* loops, back to front. Draw up to create a third loop.

5   Now that you have enough loops to work with, for each subsequent pass, draw the working end through the *two most recent* rings only, as shown in the photo.

6 Unless you are keeping the sinnet loose, it is best to tighten as you go. Always work the slack out of the third ring, which is the ring previous to the two rings you are encircling for the next loop. If you find this difficult, it's OK to tape the beginning end of the sinnet to a tabletop to keep it flat and workable.

In this tutorial, I've left the rings loose due to the fluffy material I'm working with.

7 The chain will look even more lush if you work three rings at a time instead of two.

The sinnet can be attached at the ends to create a cowl, necklace, or wool "lei."

four-ply single-strand lanyard knot

Lanyard knots are those in which the cord enters and exits the knot at opposite sides of the knot. Undoubtedly their utility runs deep and wide, but, as with most of the knots in this book, I'm drawn more to lanyards' aesthetics than function. Added to otherwise unadorned lines, they can act as small moments of visual pleasure.

This, one of the prettiest of the single-strand lanyard knots, is made from interlocked rings, as pure in its flattened state as when it's drawn up into a swirling bead.

MATERIALS

I used 3' (91 cm) of ⁵⁄₁₆" (7.5-mm) cotton braid. The knot can accommodate any type and width of cord on the softer side, although I think using stranded twist with it would make the already-swirling knot swirl even more. Man overboard.

WORKING PART

STANDING END

1 Form a loop near one end of the cord, with the working part crossing *over* the standing end.

2 Make a second loop to the right of the original: As with the first loop, the working part crosses over the standing part, and the loop is also interwoven with the first.

3 Make four more loops using the same logic, crossing each new loop over all the previous ones. In other words, each of the three loops must intersect with the original.

4 Work out the slack gradually. If you yank an end, the knot will lose its shape and you will have to start over.

5 Keep the scallops in place as you tighten.

6 From all angles, especially the side, the knot exhibits a pleasant swirling shape.

chinese button and diamond knot tassel

Building on the Single-Strand Button Knots you've learned (page 20), here are two closely related single-strand cousins: the Chinese Button (otherwise known as the "pajama knot," because its softness is comfortable to lie upon) and the Diamond Knot (otherwise known as the Knife Lanyard, Bosun's Whistle Knot, Marlinspike Lanyard, and more—after all, a knot is not a real knot unless it has twenty-seven alternate names).

 Both these knots start with a single-strand version of the classic Carrick Bend shape (which is also utilized for the Gift Knot, page 62) and differ only in how their ends are tucked and worked. Interestingly, though, the Chinese Button belongs to the button family, while the Diamond Knot belongs to the family of lanyard knots. Thus, these two are good examples of how so many knots are interrelated and spring from only a few basic forms.

MATERIALS

Here, I'm using 3' (91 cm) of 5⁄16" (7.5-mm) cotton braid, but the knots are handsome in many materials and widths of cord. I once made the Chinese Button out of surgical tubing, and I work Diamond Knots with para-cord to use as keychains.

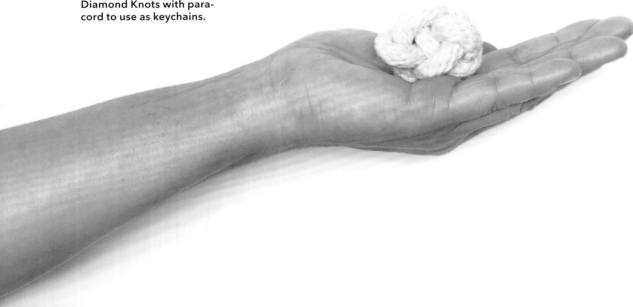

MIDPOINT

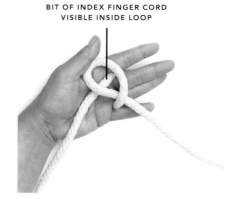

BIT OF INDEX FINGER CORD
VISIBLE INSIDE LOOP

THE CARRICK BEND

1 Bends, a huge family of knots, are those that connect two lines, yet in this case we are using a single line. Nonetheless, the Carrick Bend *shape* is the basis of the following two knots.

To form the Carrick shape in your hand, drape the midpoint of the cord around the middle and ring fingers on the back of your hand.

2 Turn the palm faceup and arrange the ends as shown, with the index finger cord on the left and the pinkie cord on the right.

3 Using the pinkie cord, as shown in the photo, make a loop with the working end emerging from *behind* the loop.

You should be able to see a bit of the index finger cord *inside* the loop. If you don't see it there, adjust the placement of the loop.

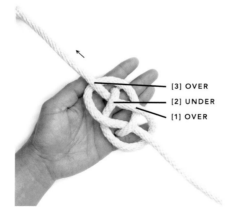

[3] OVER
[2] UNDER
[1] OVER

4 Draw the index finger cord below the loop and *behind* the pinkie cord.

5 Still working with the index finger cord, draw it upward across the loop. In doing so, you will make three crossings: [1] *over* the bottom part of the loop; [2] *under* the bit of cord inside the loop; and, finally, [3] *over* the top part of the loop. The crossing pattern is *over-under-over*.

This is the Carrick Bend shape. Nice work!

Both the **Chinese Button** and the **Diamond Knot** start with this shape.

DIAMOND-SHAPED
HOLE

THE CHINESE BUTTON

1 First, notice the diamond-shaped hole in the center of the Carrick.

Draw the bottom cord to the right of the Carrick, then enter the hole from the back and draw the cord forward through it.

2 Now do the same with the top cord by drawing it first to the left of the Carrick, then through the hole from back to front.

It will look like you gave the Carrick two ears.

3 Gather both ends together with your right hand and pull them forward through the hole, while simultaneously removing the "ring" from the back of your left hand.

LITTLE "DASH"
AT CENTER

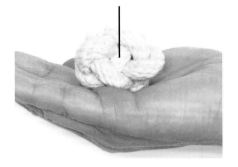

4 Hold the two legs together in your fist like a flower stem.

The knot will seem worryingly loose. This is normal.

5 Carefully work the knot snug by inching the slack out bit by bit. You may feel compelled to yank at the ends, but that may distort the knot beyond repair.

I struggled with this one several times before getting it. It helps to know how it is supposed to look when finished. Refer to the photos for top and side views. The proper Chinese Button has a little

"dash" at its top center and a pleasantly spherical shape, and the sides look latticed.

75

THE DIAMOND KNOT TASSEL

1 Make the Carrick Bend shape again as shown above (page 74).

To form the Diamond Knot, you will again be pulling the ends forward through the diamond-shaped hole, but you must first cross *over* the rope "ring" you're wearing on the back of your fingers.

In this photo, the bottom cord is drawn to the right of the Carrick, then up toward your thumb, and crossing to the left *over* the cord between index and middle fingers.

Only then do you insert it into the back of the hole and draw forward.

2 Similarly, draw the top cord to the left of the Carrick, then down toward your pinkie, and crossing over to the *right* of the rope "ring" between your pinkie and ring finger.

Only then do you insert it into the back of the hole and draw forward.

3 My favorite part: Remove the rope "ring" from the back of your hand.

Pull the "ring" to the left while simultaneously pulling the legs to the right.

4 Just by you pulling the legs and ring as shown in the previous photo, the knot will snuggle itself into shape somewhat. In order to find its final shape, though, it must still be worked as much as the Chinese Button.

if you don't love the process, don't do it

When something feels good while you're doing it, it's worth continuing. The flip side of the coin is, of course, if it doesn't feel good, stop. It's not worth your time. Why put yourself through it if it's not enjoyable? The journey is as important as the destination. I use this as a barometer for deciding when to go deep.

Back in college at San Francisco State University, I majored in filmmaking. But, unlike many of my classmates, I chose not to make a career out of it. At the time, I didn't analyze the decision; I merely thought, "I want to be involved with the thing I'm most excited by right now," which was the music scene. But recently, when answering a particularly insightful podcast host's question, I realized the actual reason I left film was because I didn't love the process. I loved the results of film-making (and still do), but that is not enough. Filmmaking is a long, drawn-out process, often taking years to reach fruition on a single work. That timeline is too long for my gratification-needing ass. Nor do I enjoy geeking out on lenses and film stock.

In contrast, carving wood feels so good. I love the way the spoon gouge slides into the walnut like butter. I love using the Shinto Saw Rasp to shape curves. Even sanding is a magical pleasure.

And when I'm designing and making large, site-specific rope installations, I love it all, every phase of the projects. I love experimenting to determine the exact right knot for the work, love the feel of rope in my hands: the comfort of cotton, the heft of manila. I love the initial excited conversations with my clients about the space in which the work will live and their hopes for the piece; I love discussing the best shooting angles with professional photographers; and I especially love hiring and working with the sassiest female assistants in each new city where I'm installing.

constrictor knot

The mighty Constrictor! When applied around a convex surface, the Constrictor is so strong and secure, and holds so tightly, that in some cases the only way to undo it is to cut it. While I have included the other knots in this book because they're beautiful in concept and/or execution, this stalwart from the family of binding knots is included for its usefulness. The Constrictor is handy as a whipping to prevent ends from fraying or a seizing to bind together two or more objects. When made from "small stuff" (thread or twine), it can rather satisfyingly bite into rope fibers.

Macramé artists will notice that the knot at first resembles the popular Clove Hitch, but they are not the same. The Constrictor, due to its additional crossings, is much stronger and relatively bulkier.

MATERIALS

In this tutorial, I am using 1' (30.5 cm) of ³⁄₁₆" (4.5-mm) cotton braid. The rule of thumb is to use a length three times the circumference of the object to be bound.

Note: The knot binds best around convex surfaces, not straight or concave faces.

STANDING END

● WORKING CORD

1 The Constrictor is simple. Lay the cord across the object (in this case, a very thick twisted rope), with the short standing end pointing up.

Make one turn around the object to the right of the standing end. Cross the working cord leftward over the standing end on the way down.

Notice the X shape.

2 Draw the working end upward behind the object and draw it left to right *in front of* the standing end.

3 Thread the working end downward under both legs of the X.

4 Tighten by pulling both ends. You can really ratchet it.

Trim the ends.

Front and back views.

ringbolt necklace

In December, when the Year of Knots was almost complete, I discovered ringbolt hitching, and quickly realized this type of knotting would become a part of my work moving forward. It was another moment—in a year of many such moments—when a knot came to me at exactly the right time, when I was skilled enough to understand it and open enough to marvel.

But before we discuss ringbolt hitching, what are hitches, generally? Hitches are knots that attach to objects. They differ from loop knots, though. A loop knot holds its shape and its integrity—the properties that make it a knot— whether or not it is attached to or encircling an object, but a hitch will likely capsize if the object around which it was made is removed. Hitches require something to attach to. There are several hundred hitches described by Clifford Ashley in *The Ashley Book of Knots*: hitches with perpendicular pull or with parallel pull, hitches that slide (such as nooses), hitches for placing over hooks, slipped temporary hitches for belaying objects, and many more.

Ringbolt hitching originated as protection against chafing for metal rings aboard ship or onshore. The idea is to serve (cover with rope) the entirety of the ring, and because the ring's outside circumference is larger than its inner, the knotting fills any outside gaps.

The popular Ringbolt Hitch pattern worked here is also called keckling or cackling. It consists of alternating left and right Single Hitches (also known as Lark's Head or Cow Hitch knots) in sequence around the ring. Obsessed as I am with the purity of the circle shape, it wasn't two minutes after learning this hitch that I felt compelled to make something with it. I already had wood rings for macramé plant hangers . . . and the Ringbolt Necklace was born.

MATERIALS

12′ (3.7 m) of ¼″ (6-mm) cotton braid

3″ (7.5-cm) diameter wood (or metal) ring

Bent-nose pliers

In addition to cotton, I make the necklace with polypropylene braid because I like the soft, licorice-like shine of synthetic fiber; you can also use any other cord. The design is so simple, it invites variation. The ring can be metal or other material, as long as it is substantial.

KNOTS

RINGBOLT HITCH
(alternating left and right Single Hitches, aka Lark's Head/Cow Hitch)

TRIPLE ENGLISH KNOT

1 Middle the cord and pop the bight up through the ring, front to back.

2 Pull the midpoint forward and down below the ring, then pull the legs downward to tighten.

3 Macramé artists will recognize this as the Lark's Head Knot.

   We'll continue making this knot shape around the circumference of the ring, with the left working cord traveling up the left side of the ring, and the right working cord climbing up the right side.

4 The Lark's Head shape is usually made in one quick motion, both hitches at once, but because we are now working with a single cord, it is more accurate to say we are making a pair of left and right Single Hitches, one after the other.

   Insert the right working cord into the hole, front to back, and draw it forward to the left of itself, creating a Single Hitch.

   Pull the hitch very tight. Rope, being composed of fibers, will inevitably loosen over time, so get it as tight as possible now.

5 Make another Single Hitch, this time reversing it: Insert the right working cord into the hole, *back to front*, and draw it downward under itself, thus making a Single Hitch that is the mirror image of the previous one.

6 Pull the second Single Hitch tight.

Look at your knot and notice you now have what looks like two Lark's Heads.

7 Continue making the same pairs of hitches with the right working cord until you have five Lark's Heads, as shown.

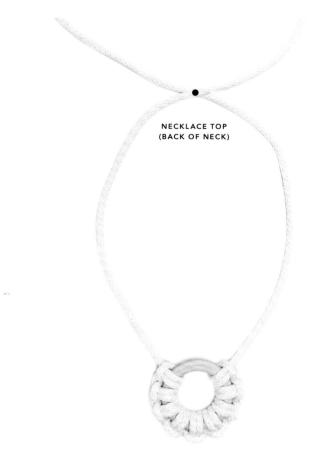

**NECKLACE TOP
(BACK OF NECK)**

8 Complete the ringbolt hitching up the left side of the ring using the left working cord.

Stop when you have nine or ten Lark's Heads, or you can knot until the hitches meet at top of ring, thereby, covering the entire ring. It's your aesthetic decision.

Use bent-nose pliers to tighten the hitches again, really, really tight.

To join the necklace, measure it around your neck and cross the working cords at your desired longest length. Prepare to make the sliding Triple English Knot.

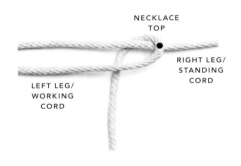

LEFT LEG/
WORKING
CORD

NECKLACE
TOP

RIGHT LEG/
STANDING
CORD

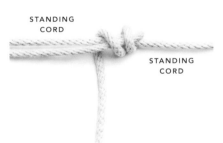

STANDING
CORD

STANDING
CORD

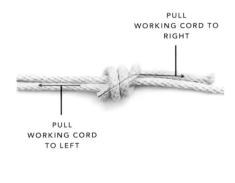

PULL
WORKING CORD TO
RIGHT

PULL
WORKING CORD
TO LEFT

9 The **Triple English Knot** is a bend, meaning it connects two cords, and its inherent tension allows for length adjustment. When I learned this knot, it was as if one of the secrets of the universe had finally been revealed to me.

Lay the necklace leg ends horizontally parallel and traveling in opposite directions. The standing cord from the right is above; the working cord from the left is below.

Using the working cord, wrap a slightly loose single turn around the standing cord front to back and emerging from behind both legs.

10 With the same working cord, wrap two more similar turns around both cords, ending with the working cord traveling downward from behind.

Hold the turns in place with your fingers. They should be slightly loose, not snug.

11 This is the tricky part. Feed the working cord from the left to the right through the inside of *all three* turns. In doing so, the working cord will run parallel to the standing cord inside the coils, and will emerge *above* the standing cord.

Using your fingers, work the slack out of the turns so they are tight, then tug on the two parts of the working cord, pulling them apart as tightly as you can. Seriously, you want this knot incredibly tight.

There's no need to tug on the standing cord.

12 Flip the entire necklace over horizontally so that the knot you just made is on the left. What *was* the standing cord now becomes the new working cord, and it is traveling to the right below the standing part.

Make the Triple English Knot again, this time using the new working cord to make turns around the standing cord. The

instructions are identical: Start with the working cord below and parallel to the standing part, then coil it over and around the standing part three times, emerging from behind both cords.

The photo shows the completed second half of the Triple English Knot, before tightening.

13 When both halves of the Triple English Knot are made correctly, they'll nest together neatly.

Here are back and front views.

14 The two halves of the knot can be slid apart to shorten the necklace.

the
lightbulb

ne January morning, not long after New Year's Day, I was cleaning up my backyard woodworking studio and thinking about the year ahead. I was exhausted; I had survived the Christmas retail season, and I had already begun making freeform macramé wall hangings to balance the repetitiveness of my beloved Helix Lights, but when I looked at the wall pieces objectively, I thought the work was too much like everyone else's.

Most macramé comprises the same three or four knots repeated in varying combinations and patterns. Indeed, macramé knots are a small subset within the family of ornamental knots, which is itself a subset of the larger world of knots. There are several thousand documented knots, and mathematicians theorize that many more are possible. So while I found macramé blissful, I also felt constrained by the knots macramé artists commonly use. It's like playing the guitar. If you know only three chords, well, you can play the Ramones. But if you want to play Jimi Hendrix or Joni Mitchell, you've got to learn *all* the chords. Or, to use an art analogy, it's like being a painter with only three colors on your palette.

So on that morning, it came to me all at once: I needed more knots. I needed more tools to reflect multifaceted me.

I'd often heard about so-called lightbulb-over-the-head moments, but thought that if one hadn't happened to me by the age of forty-eight, then they really were just the stuff of comic books and movies. So I was thrilled and very surprised to have such a moment. Suddenly, a program had unfurled itself in my mind:

To expand my repertoire, I would learn and make one new knot each and every day of 2016. The kernel of the idea was practical: learn a lot of knots. But the magic of the idea was the way it would work. I would frame the goal into a structured practice—a daily ritual. It even had a name: the Year of Knots.

I knew myself well enough to know that this idea would work in my life. It was a series of bite-size assignments over a long period of time. **It wasn't too much nor too little: I could sustain it for the duration. It added an exciting element of discovery and newness to a creative life** I was already pretty happy with, and would satiate my desire for something fresh, but without pulling my focus away from the task at hand.

I've always loved being in a "learning phase"; I think it's an appealingly humble state of mind. With curiosity as my guide, I would learn a new knot a day, using those books I had collected but never really studied.

I have long admired conceptual projects that unfold over a period of time, like Japanese artist On Kawara's date paintings, along with artist-conceived constructs for creativity, such as Brian Eno and Peter Schmidt's Oblique Strategies cards. Years before, I had even carried out one of Yoko Ono's instruction paintings—*Painting to Hammer a Nail*—by doing just that into a wooden board every day; the piece still hangs in my home.

That moment. **Have you ever had such an epiphany? It felt like lightning (or the muse) had struck.** It was a pure flash of clarity, bringing together process, aesthetics, learning, everything I'd been before and everything I wanted to be, all in one clean plan. Filmmaker and artist David Lynch describes such an experience as submerging in a large, boundless sea where ideas swim, ready for capturing. There are many small ideas, but the big ones—the big fish—only come around occasionally and you have to be ready. I felt incredibly fertile, buzzing with energy.

bryr button

For a collaboration with San Francisco clog maker Isobel Schofield, I developed an original, four-strand button knot that fit these requirements: The knot had to be compact enough to look proportionally pleasing on a shoe, sturdy enough to withstand frequent handling without distorting, simple enough that I could make many pairs, and pretty enough that a cool girl would want to wear it.

As a final touch, we gathered the eight legs of the button together and deliberately unraveled them for a decorative fringe.

I loved this collaboration.

MATERIALS

**Four 3' (91-cm) strands of ¼"
(6-mm) cotton braid**

**Rubber band, paper tape, or
"small stuff" (see page 17)
for seizing (see page 114)**

SKILLS

The Bryr Button comprises two rounds of *crowning* and one round of *tucks*, both of which are explained below. Crowning seems intimidating at first, but it's a simple concept. And with multistrand buttons, the only thing to remember is that you will make the same action for every strand in the knot. Therefore, because the Bryr Button is made from four strands, you will perform each step four times, once on each strand.

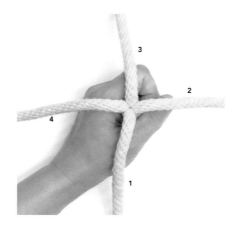

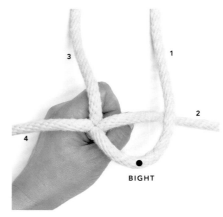

BIGHT

1. Gather the four lines together.

   About 4" (10 cm) from an end, seize the strands into a "stem" with the rubber band or paper tape, or make a Constrictor Knot (page 78) with the small stuff.

2. Hold the stem in your hand and arrange the four cords equidistant from each other.

3. **To crown is to cross over in sequence.** In this case, we will cross each cord *over* the neighboring cord to its right (counterclockwise).

   Cross cord 1 over cord 2, its neighbor to the right, as shown in the photo.

   Leave a loose bight (open curve) in cord 1. This should be easy to do when your hand is held over a tabletop, as shown in the photo.

   Tip: When you are comfortable enough to make this knot in your hand *without* a tabletop, it will be a little harder to keep the bight open and in place without collapsing. To do so, draw cord 1 down to the stem after you cross it over cord 2, and hold cord 1 lightly against the stem. At first, this will seem confusing, but it is a good way to keep a bight open.

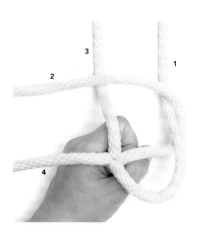

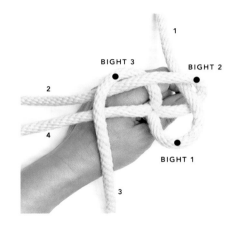

---

4 Continue crowning in a counterclockwise direction, each cord passing over its neighbor to its *right*.

Here, cord 2 crowns cord 3 (and, in doing so, also crosses over cord 1).

5 Here, cord 3 crowns cord 4, also crossing over cord 2.

Make sure to keep the bights open and in place, like flower petals.

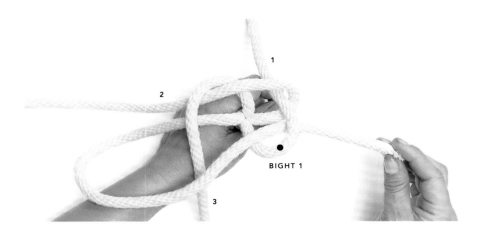

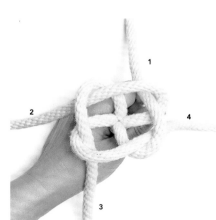

---

6 Pay special attention to cord 4, the last in the crown. In order for cord 4 to crown its neighbor to the right (cord 1), it must *enter* bight 1.

This last strand is always the most potentially confusing part of the crown. It is easy to "lose" that first bight, and then you're left wondering where to put cord 4.

Stay positive! The knot is worth it.

Four properly crowned strands, before working snug.

EMPTY SPACE
INSIDE
THE BIGHT

7 Draw all the cords together firmly. When you've tightened them sufficiently, tension will "lock" the crown into place. It will feel right and look good.

8 Crown all the strands to the right a second time. The photo shows the completed second crown in its loose form.

9 This second crown will become part of the button's rim, so do *not* tighten it completely. Work out the slack, but leave small, loose bights with visible spaces you can see through.

Notice the empty space inside each of the open bights.

Now, we'll tuck to the right. To begin tucking, choose any strand.

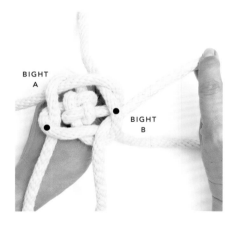

BIGHT A

BIGHT B

10 Tuck the strand down into the bight to its right, crossing over the cord that's already in the bight.

For example, in the photo, the working strand is traveling out of bight A and tucked down into bight B.

If your knot looks like the photo above, congratulations!

11 Pull the tucked cord all the way down into the bight, so it becomes part of the rim.

12 Continue tucking each of the remaining three strands counterclockwise.

13 When all four cords have been tucked, the rim will look scalloped, as in this photo.

14 Work each section of the rim snug. This cannot be accomplished by only tugging the ends; each rim strand must be worked bit by bit so that the button does not distort.

The completed Bryr Button will hold its shape and the rim will feel secure.

15 Remove the rubber band or other temporary seizing.

Trim the four long legs so they match the four short ones, and gather all to one side. Use your palm to flatten the button against the tabletop.

If desired, fray the ends for fringe.

If you haven't got a pair of killer clogs to attach this to, I think it would make a nice pin.

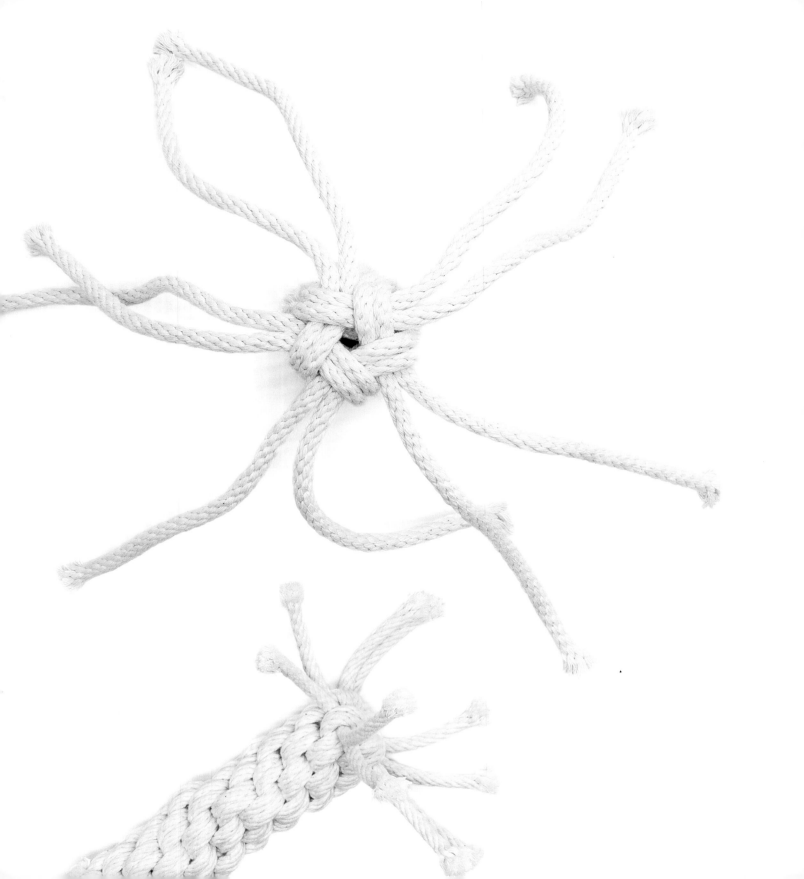

five-sided parallel strand reverse crown sinnet

I can think of no better way to practice crowning than with this beautiful, solid, substantial crown sinnet. Don't be intimidated by its name. This is simply a braided chain of ten strands worked in five pairs. Each crown layer alternates moving clockwise or counterclockwise, which gives the sinnet a handsome vertical link surface.

When several of these are grouped together, I think they look like sea anemones.

MATERIALS

**Ten 3' (91-cm) strands of ³⁄₁₆"
(4.5-mm) cotton braid will
make a 10" (25-cm) sinnet**

**Rubber band or "small stuff"
(see page 17) for seizing (see
page 114)**

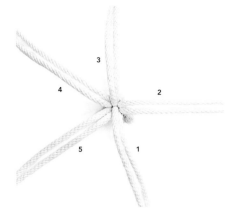

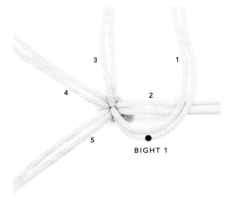

1 Seize the strands together at one end with a rubber band or, if you're feeling particularly badass, a tight Constrictor Knot (page 78) or Common Whipping (page 27).

2 Divide the strands into pairs and arrange so the five parts are equidistant from each other.

For sake of simplicity, I have photographed this knot on a tabletop, but once you understand crowning, it's easier to give this sinnet room to grow by making it in your hand, holding the stem in one fist.

3 Begin crowning counterclockwise. Cross each pair of cords *over* its neighboring pair to the right.

Here, pair 1 crowns pair 2.

Leave a loose bight (open curve) in pair 1 near the stem. This should be easy to do on a tabletop, but if you are making the knot in your hand, draw pair 1 down to the stem after crossing it over pair 2, and hold it lightly with your fingers against the stem to keep its bight in place without collapsing.

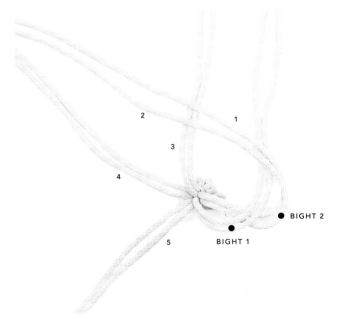

4 Continue crowning to the right. Here, pair 1 has already crowned pair 2, so now pair 2 crowns pair 3. (In doing so, pair 2 also crosses over pair 1. Let that happen.)

Make sure to keep the bights open and in place, like flower petals.

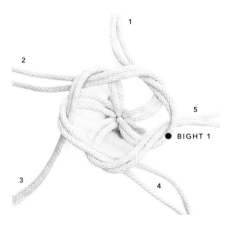

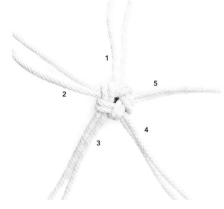

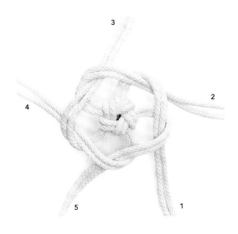

5 Continue crowning to the right, moving counterclockwise.

In each case, the pair that is crowning will cross over the neighbor to its right. (And again, in doing so, it will also cross over the pair that just crossed it.)

Take special care with pair 5, the last pair of strands. In order for it to crown pair 1, it must *enter* bight 1.

6 Draw all the cords snug. When you've tightened sufficiently, tension will "lock" the shape into place.

You'll see a beautiful pentagon.

If any cord is twisted with its paired sister, smooth them out so they're parallel. No twisted sisters.

7 Now for something new: Crown all the strands to the *left*. In other words, crown in a clockwise direction.

Your first move is to crown pair 1 over pair 5, its clockwise neighbor. Then, pair 5 crowns leftward over pair 4, and so on. Be sure that the last strand—pair 2—enters the final bight (bight 1).

As each crown layer is complete, tighten it quite firmly.

8 Grow the sinnet by repeating the crowning in alternate left and right layers. The sinnet will feel substantial and dense in the hand. It will display an attractive, rounded pentagonal cross section with the surface "chain links" moving straight up the sinnet.

what's your
project?

**N**othing would make me happier than to hear you are going to embark on your own yearlong commitment, or #100DayProject, or whatever time frame feels right for you. However, I don't want you to struggle, so it's important that you choose the idea well.

MAKE SPACE FOR THE ANSWER TO COME. I call it a lightbulb moment, but in reality, an idea that at first seems to have appeared out of nowhere is actually the result of a longer, intentional process of living in a way such that you're *receptive* to the big idea. Don't force it. Some people reach such states via meditation. For me, it was the result of intentionally setting myself on a course of exploration.

The stories in this book illustrate that. I had to go deep into macramé in order to realize the form has its limitations, and had to endure a couple of years of hectic holiday retail seasons in order to conclude I didn't want to make products. All those experiences led to the Year of Knots.

YOU DON'T HAVE TO PULL AN IDEA OUT OF THIN AIR. Your thing—your breakthrough idea—is probably tantalizingly close, at once familiar and yet with substantial parts unknown. Keep doing what you're already doing, and kick it up a notch. Remember the author and main character in *Julie & Julia*? She was already cooking well every day, but learning all the recipes in *Mastering the Art of French Cooking* took her to the next level. As for me, I had been working long enough with knots to know I wanted to tie more, and that there were thousands I had *not* yet made. (This was, ironically, reassuring: I would never run out of material over the course of the year.)

SET LEARNING AS YOUR PRIMARY GOAL. Despite the fact that this point is listed third, it is my number-one piece of advice. **For maximum life transformation potential, choose something to learn.** The world is filled with daily art projects that faltered because the artist lost inspiration or pressured herself to reinvent the wheel every day. Nobody can paint a new *Mona Lisa* each morning or find fresh inspiration every single day, so don't set that level of creative expectation for yourself.

Instead, approach the project as an opportunity to *self-educate*. If you're informed enough to know how much you *don't* know, that's your opportunity.

Of course, if you decide your project is to repeatedly do something you already know how to do, simply to get into the habit of making, there's nothing wrong with that. But you might get bored. I think that if you're going to spend a year, or one hundred days, doing anything, the rewards should be more substantive. The accumulation of knowledge and proficiency is what will give the project richer dimension and level up your game. Aim high.

KEEP IT BITE-SIZE. This is just practical. If it takes ten or twenty minutes, you'll never get overwhelmed. Instead, you will look forward to it. It never failed to amaze me how little time and effort it took to do something that made me feel so good for the rest of my day. If your art involves bigger projects that require more time to complete, consider breaking the process down into small daily steps.

DO SOMETHING THAT'S A LITTLE SCARY. Fear springs from the unknown, but a year-long project is inevitably going to have some unknowns, no matter how much you prepare—so embrace them. Otherwise, there's no potential for growth. If you choose something you already know how to do, and try to do that very same thing each day, you won't feel fear, but you also won't learn anything.

FOLLOW YOUR CURIOSITY. To some, curiosity feels squishy and amorphous, but it will not lead you astray. Your curiosity is a finely tuned barometer. When it asks questions like "Why?" and "What would happen if . . . ," your project can be as simple as the journey of answering those questions. As Steve Jobs said: "[H]ave the courage to follow your heart and intuition. They somehow already know what you truly want to become. Everything else is secondary."

STRIP DOWN IN ORDER TO OPEN UP. Self-imposed restrictions are not necessarily confining; they can be liberating. They provide clarity so the road is clear. For example, by limiting myself to white rope photographed on a white background, I freed myself from having to think about color and presentation, which allowed me to hone in on each knot's structure and line—the parts I was most interested in.

Put another way: Elements should be used intentionally. Keeping secondary elements minimized and consistent allows the work to communicate more clearly.

BE REALISTIC. Consider your time constraints, the physical space where you do the work, your process, the money and supplies required, etc. Your project will make sense on every level when you've synthesized practicality with your passion. This will allow you to practice in a way that fits into your life.

DON'T WORRY ABOUT WHAT IT WILL LOOK LIKE AT THE END OF THE PROJECT. You can't know that, so don't waste any time thinking about it. I promise you, over the course of the commitment, good things will happen that you didn't anticipate. Momentum will gather, your world will expand, and, as Joseph Campbell pointed out, "doors will open where you didn't know they were going to be." When I set out to learn a knot every day for a year, I had no idea that when the year was over, the knots would hold together as a single work of art. I couldn't have known.

You will find the work's meaning, and your purpose, over the course of the project's life. The daily commitment will ensure your art will unconsciously evolve in your mind even when you're not actively doing it in the moment; larger meaning and bigger projects will suggest themselves to you seemingly effortlessly. In the meantime, just do.

rib stitch hitch

Of the many, *many* decorative hitches one can make around, well, almost anything, this is one of the most handsome. It can cover a ring, in which case you'd have a cousin to the **Ringbolt Necklace** (page 80), but the hitch can also be used as a covering for cylindrical or oblong objects, such as a bottle, boat fender, or more (let your imagination run wild), by making the hitching in long, connected vertical rows, like a net.

MATERIALS

Rope that is pleasingly proportional to the width of the object to be knotted around. (It really can be any width—it's up to the knotter's aesthetic and intentions.)

Object to knot around

Rubber band or "small stuff" (see page 17) for seizing (optional; see page 114)

In this photo, I used 8' (2.4 m) of ¼" (6-mm) cotton braid around a wood rail to make seven hitches. Since I don't know the circumference of the object you'll be hitching to, my advice is simply to use more than you think you'll need (weirdly, this usually ends up being just the right amount). Measure the circumference of the object, think of the number of hitches you want, which is itself a function of the width of your rope, and so on.

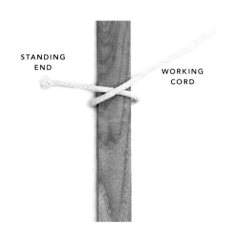

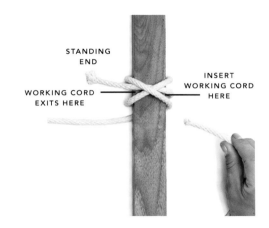

STANDING END

WORKING CORD

STANDING END

WORKING CORD EXITS HERE

INSERT WORKING CORD HERE

1 The knot is worked downward (toward you) in this tutorial, so start at the upper end of your desired placement.

With one end of the cord, make a Single Hitch (page 82) around the rail. The working cord crosses over its standing end and holds it against the rail.

2 Draw the working cord behind the rail and cross over the front of the knot again, forming an X shape.

Draw the working cord behind the rail again, coming to rest on the left, below the knot.

3 Notice the X shape, which is holding down the standing end.

Grasp the working cord, draw it to the right over the rail, and prepare to insert it into the *right side* of the X.

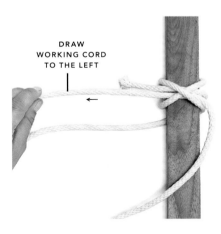
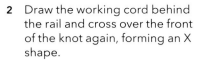
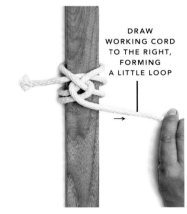

DRAW WORKING CORD TO THE LEFT

DRAW WORKING CORD TO THE RIGHT, FORMING A LITTLE LOOP

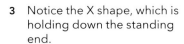

4 Tuck the working cord right to left *underneath* both bottom legs of the X, between the X and the rail, and below the standing end.

5 Pull the working cord leftward to draw it all the way through the X, then draw it toward the right, which will form a little loop in the middle of the knot.

This little loop is the first Rib Stitch Hitch.

6 Continue the simple pattern of drawing the cord leftward behind the rail, then across the front of the rail to tuck under the X from *right to left*, and so on.

Repeat until the Rib Stitch Hitching is the desired length.

The ends may be trimmed and hidden behind the hitch if it will not be seen from behind, tucked under the turns, or seized against the rail.

zigzag hitch

This type of knot covering is also called coachwhipping. As an ornamental application, the Zigzag Hitch is as beautiful on straight and curved lengths as it is on a ring. I recently applied it to thick, rounded rattan to spectacular effect. I like it for the beautiful harmony of the three lines traveling in parallel and the plush cushion of their angled layers.

      The Zigzag Hitch is simply three strands running parallel to each other and hitched alternately left and right for as long as you wish. Experiment with additional strands, or strands of different widths.

MATERIALS

Three 6' (1.8-m) strands of ¼" (6-mm) cotton braid make the 8" (20-cm) hitching shown here, which has 30 individual hitches

Wood rail, or other oblong surface to hitch around

Rubber band or "small stuff" (see page 17) for seizing (optional; see page 114)

Bent-nose pliers

 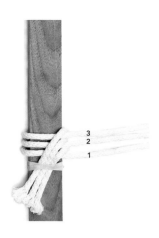 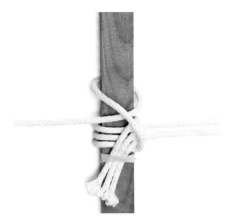

1   Begin the Zigzag Hitch with a Single Hitch toward the right around the rail. Because the Zigzag Hitch is worked upward, position this first hitch at the bottom end of your desired placement.

2   Using the second and third cords, make two more identical Single Hitches above the first.

Secure the standing ends with a rubber band or temporary Common Whipping (page 27).

Tighten each of the hitches so they are snug.

3   Starting with the cord 1 again, draw its working end to the left across the front of the rail, behind the rail, and under itself to make another Single Hitch. The working cord exits the hitch toward the left.

 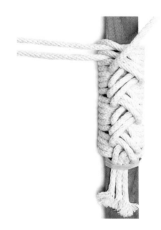 

4   Again, form two more hitches sequentially above the first one, using the cords 2 and 3.

Draw all three hitches snugly against the rail and against each other. The diagonals should be parallel and touching.

5   Continue forming the set of three hitches alternately toward the right and then the left, always working all three cords as a set and in sequence from bottom to top.

6   When you've reached the desired length, notice that the diagonals are likely a bit messy. Tidying them up will make a big difference in appearance here. Tighten the hitches as you tidy them. Bent-nose pliers are perfect for this step.

zigzag hitch

105

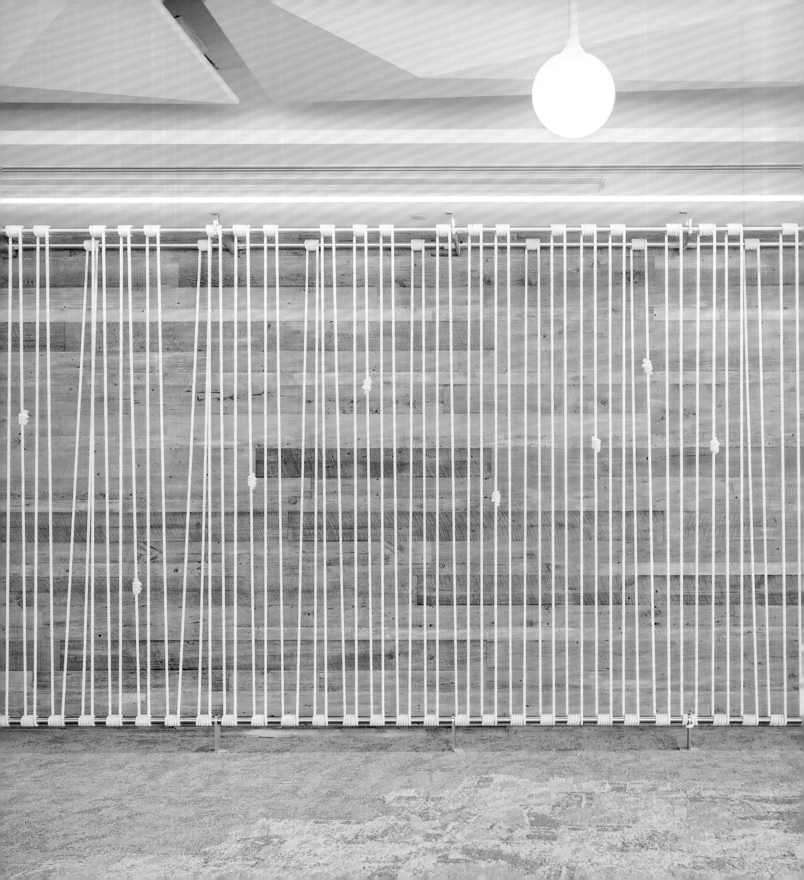

the
practice:
i walk
the line

So the same day I had the light-bulb moment, I taught myself four knots to catch up to the calendar (it was January 4), and with that, the Year of Knots was born. Then, with my purpose laid out in front of me, it was off to the races.

I started each day's session by paging through my library of reference books and choosing a knot to learn. At first, I chose randomly. With the whole world of knots at my fingertips, and feeling like a beginner all over again, I didn't feel the need to be organized. If a knot looked intriguing, or extra pretty, or was the most basic version of a whole family of knots I knew I'd get to later, I made it.

I took inspiration from the writer's practice of beginning each morning by picking up the plot where she has purposely left it the day before, knowing what will happen next. It allows her to plunge into the work without delay.

With similar aplomb, I dove into my daily Year of Knots task; indeed, **it didn't feel like work at all, but a moment I had gifted myself. I knew that every single day I would learn something useful and make something beautiful.** The daily practice allowed me to go on mini-excursions, with consecutive stretches of days devoted to learning loop knots and the crazy animal-ness of splices. I'd start with the simplest version of, say, a button knot (page 20), made with a single strand, then a week later I'd be constructing one with eight strands, a task I once would have found unthinkably complex.

Following each daily knot practice, I would spend of the rest of my time making commissioned pieces, producing Helix Lights, and developing a new line of wall hangings, the Circuit Boards, that I was really excited about, and all of which sold. Sales and commissions are great: Not only do they pay the bills, but also they allow me to befriend and collaborate with cool art collectors, interior designers, and architects over a shared aesthetic. However, commissions are usually based on *past* work that a client has seen and wants, and it's dangerously easy to coast on making the same thing over and over. If I only made proven sellers and commissions based on past work, I'd be repeating myself. I wouldn't grow. The Year of Knots, on the other hand, I was doing for its own sake. It was the only part of my day that was reliably new, unknown, and full of undiscovered potential. And therein lies a fantastic lesson:

The only one who will push you forward is you. Only your self-designed commitment will force you to do something new every day.

To further my clarity of seeing, I drastically simplified all elements other than the *line*. A principle learned during my career at Apple is that when unnecessary elements are stripped away, you are left with the essence of the thing. Beauty comes from that purity. The object speaks more clearly. As legendary industrial designer Dieter Rams pointed out: "Good design is as little design as possible: less, but better—because it concentrates on the essential aspects, and the products are not burdened with non-essentials. Back to purity, back to simplicity."

For instance, since exploring color was not my objective, I made the knots exclusively out of white cotton rope. When a knot occasionally demanded a second cord (such as

with *bends*, the family of knots that unite two cords), I used a navy or a black rope to accentuate how the lines interact with each other. Similarly, I de-emphasized scale and texture by photographing each knot alone on a white background, the light coming from the same direction each time.

Posting a daily photo turned out to be a surprisingly pleasant activity. I used iPhone photo-editing apps to make each image consistent, no matter what the light conditions were like. I delighted in learning photography basics, and a professional photographer friend showed me how to bounce light with sheets of white Formica. Admiring my progress via my Instagram feed, even after only one month with a mere thirty knots done, felt gratifying. I'm fascinated by the concept of process, and especially as it relates to the performance of a daily activity, and I encourage you to use documentation to measure progress and encourage advancement toward a goal. **The slow accumulation of my knots represented time spent, devotion to the craft, and unfolding discovery.**

And then, a couple of months into the project, as I mounted each knot to the growing collection on my wall, I suddenly realized that they were holding together as a single piece.

I hadn't anticipated this. By the end of the year, the Year of Knots was not only a huge collection—it was art.

spectacle knot

The Korean *maedeup* knotter from whom I learned this beauty calls it the Spectacle Knot, after the way two of them tied in sequence resemble eyeglasses. It is also called Caisson Ceiling Knot, Plafond Knot (*plafond* is French for "ceiling"), and more.

As with so many knots, no matter how many names and diverse origin stories across cultures exist, and no matter how many methods there are to make it, the knot itself is the same, written in the universal language of the line.

The Spectacle Knot is advanced: It may take you a couple of tries to get it. Do not despair. When done properly, the knot is flat and identical on both sides, exhibiting a clean square-within-a-square design. I like to secure it with racking turns (sequential figure 8 shapes) in a luxe gold thread to hold the legs together.

The Spectacle can be made with a variety of large- and small-diameter cords, but I do recommend, because the knot is so busy, that you make it with braid or another smooth line. 5/16" (7.5-mm) cotton braid is what I find most pleasing and adequately proportioned to be used as a handsome tassel on a tote bag. The thicker the rope, the more visual impact this knot will have.

MATERIALS

6' (1.8 m) of 5/16" (7.5-mm) cotton braid

6 to 8' (1.8 to 2.4 m) of embroidery thread or other "small stuff" (see page 17)

Needle

KNOTS

SPECTACLE KNOT

SEIZING WITH RACKING TURNS

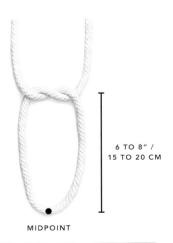

6 TO 8" /
15 TO 20 CM

MIDPOINT

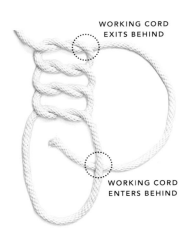

WORKING CORD
EXITS BEHIND

WORKING CORD
ENTERS BEHIND

1 Find the midpoint of your rope and tie a Half Knot 6 to 8" (15 to 20 cm) above it, forming a loop.

(This shape—the Half Knot atop the loop—is also called the Overhand Knot; see page 22.)

Tip: The 6 to 8" (15 to 20 cm) loop should look longer than you want the eventual tassel's loop to be. In the process of making the knot, the loop will grow shorter.

2 Tie three more identical Half Knots above the first, for a total of four.

Make sure they are identical; don't alternate which end of the rope goes first.

3 Look at the right working cord. Notice whether it emerges from *behind* or in *front* of the last Half Knot you made.

Thread the right working cord similarly *behind* or in *front* of the bottom loop.

In this photo, the right working cord is emerging from *behind* the last Half Knot, so it enters the bottom loop similarly from *behind*.

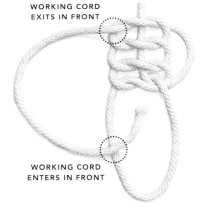

WORKING CORD
EXITS IN FRONT

WORKING CORD
ENTERS IN FRONT

4 Carefully feed the working cord upward through the centers of all four Half Knots (the centers of the knots themselves, not just the loops).

You will have to slightly pull apart each Half Knot to feed the working cord through its center.

Draw up loosely.

5 Do the same with the left working cord, applying the same *behind/ front* rule.

In this photo, the left working cord is emerging from in *front* of the last Half Knot, so it enters the bottom loop similarly from the *front*.

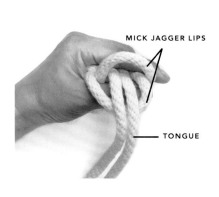

MICK JAGGER LIPS

TONGUE

6 Carefully feed the left working cord upward through the centers of all four Half Knots.

It will run parallel to the right working cord.

Draw up the cord so there's some looseness but not too much slack, like the photo shows.

Looks like lungs!

7 Pick up the knot and look at it from above, where the ends emerge.

Notice the "mouth" and "lips" surrounding the "tongue" ends. (It's a very Rolling Stones moment.)

8 Pull the lips apart and peel them—just like a banana—all the way down toward the bottom loop and below the four Half Knots, as if you're peeling a whole banana in one step.

It will feel like a very dramatic move. It *is* dramatic, but everything's going to be OK.

Let go of the lips.

9 Return to the top of the knot and notice that you've revealed a second pair of lips.

Peel these down, too—just like an entire banana—all the way below the first pair of lips.

10 Lay the knot on the tabletop.

Your knot will look like a big mess. This is normal.

11 To work the knot into shape, gently tug simultaneously on *diagonally opposite* legs. In this photo, I'm tugging on the upper-left leg (part of the loop) and lower-right leg at the same time.

Give them a couple of tugs, then switch to the other pair of diagonally opposite legs. The cords will move fractions of an inch with each tug. This is normal. Don't force it. Keep alternating legs.

The square-within-a-square shape should reveal itself soon after you start tugging at the knot. Have courage! It took me forever to train my eyes to "see" the emerging squares.

12 When no more slack is coming out via gentle tugs on the diagonally opposite legs, you must then pick up the knot and work the slack out bit by bit with your fingers, each time working a different section of cord.

While working the knot into shape, flip it often.

The knot should look like the photo, and be identical on both sides.

13 To give the Spectacle Knot a polished finish, seize the ends together with *racking turns* made of "small stuff." Racking turns alternate around each leg in a figure 8 pattern, same as in the Multiple Figure 8 Knot (page 28).

Tip: Too many racking turns with thin thread can get tedious. It is more efficient to fold the thread in half at its midpoint, then insert the *midpoint* into the eye of the needle. You will effectively have quadrupled the line and be turning four threads at a time.

Stick the needle through one of the ropes, leaving an 1"- (2.5-cm-) long tail (which will get covered up by the turns).

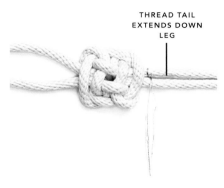

THREAD TAIL
EXTENDS DOWN
LEG

14 Arrange the tail so it is extending down one of the legs leading away from the Spectacle Knot and toward the rope end.

Wrap the small stuff around the two legs in a figure 8 pattern, first around one leg and then the other, then repeating.

You won't need to use the needle during this part; use your fingers to manipulate the thread.

15 I get a lot of satisfaction out of laying the threads neatly parallel next to each other.

Continue the figure-8-shaped racking turns until the seizing is the size desired.

Most or all of the thread tail will be covered by the racking turns.

16 When the seizing is the size you like, run the needle up under all the turns and out near where you started, close to the Spectacle Knot.

Trim the ends.

17 I love the Spectacle Knot as a bag tassel, but it's also chic as a necklace.

Bag by Agnes Baddoo

four rich things the year of knots gave me

The project had started out simply, but as it unfolded throughout the year, I had what writer Eudora Welty calls a "continuous thread of revelation," each one richer and more interesting than the last.

THE STATE OF FLOW

As I made each new knot, I had the palpable sense I was tapping into a larger consciousness of creative energy. It turned out that learning one knot a day, *as the first thing I did every day*, was a great approach, because it was an entry to the "state of flow." I had heard of the concept of flow, and it sounded like a great space to be in, but it had eluded me until now. It's the mental state where you are immersed in a feeling of blissful productivity, happily pushing at the limits of your abilities without fear of failure, where cares and distractions fall away, and the activity becomes its own reward. (I encourage you to seek out more information on the flow state and its other fascinating character-istics, as I haven't mentioned them all here.)

When you find true purpose organically, the flow state just happens naturally. When you're performing an activity for its own sake, where the pleasure is intrinsic, you can achieve it. But if you're driven by other motives, like profit, or external approval, or following a trend, you won't find flow. You can't fake it.

My experiences of flow carried me, whenever I would set about the ritual, throughout the entire Year of Knots. And now that I know the bliss of being in flow, I never want to go without it again.

ART SCHOOL

Why knots, of all things? Why do I love them so much? I already knew I was all about elevating the everyday in terms of products, and this was certainly that—but to use a fine-art term, I finally realized that my obsession was with *the line*. Immersion in knotting had become my art school.

As any art student knows (although I didn't go to art school, so I had to look it up on Wikipedia!), the line is one of the seven building-block elements of art. (The others are color, shape, form, value, space, and texture.) And it's the one that most fascinates me. The seed of the Year of Knots was self-education, but **within a couple of months, I realized that there was also something deeper going on.** I began to discover, define, and articulate my aesthetic. I realized that what I have to offer the world is art that communicates clarity about functional knots as beautifully designed objects.

Ever the good Chinese girl, I embraced the role of student and came to the project each day with "beginner's mind," an attitude of openness and curiosity. Zen teacher Shunryu Suzuki pointed out that "In the beginner's mind there are many possibilities, but in the expert's there are few." So, beginner's mind kept me free from the self-limiting attitude that a knotting expert, who arguably knows *too* much, might bring. I rarely got slowed down by "proper" methodologies, errors experts might perceive, or nomenclature arguments (the very same knot can have several names, depending on who you're talking to . . . and don't get me started on the Half Hitch/Single Hitch debate).

A HISTORY LESSON

With decades-old manuals and handbooks as my guides, the knots became a history lesson. Aside from the family of ornamental knots,

the vast majority of knots are functional, and evolved to perform specific tasks for the fisherman, the weaver, the rock climber, the rigger, the farmer, or, most often, the sailor. I delight in learning knots' context in nautical life, the material and physical properties of rope, and how for any given situation there's a knot that is right while all the others are wrong. Across histories, cultures, and oceans, knots have made their way to those who found them useful. Recently, the centuries-old "talking knots"—or quipu—of South American Andean societies have been studied and decoded, as have other knotted string devices from Hawai'ian and Chinese cultures.

MY NEW LANGUAGE

In two senses, the Year of Knots gave me a new language. First, the technical jargon of knotting is literally a language unto itself, and, being a lifelong lover of subcultures, I always try to properly use its colorful terms—such as reeve, flake, frapping, worming, marlingspike, cockscomb—whose specificity allows for precise communication. And even if they don't use the same names for them, the sailor from Africa and the sailor from Asia tie the same knots—they speak the language of knots.

No matter what form your creativity takes, I suspect your path will similarly lead you to the satisfaction of building a language from a beloved pursuit. The more I delighted in learning the language of knots, the closer I got to my second, and more important, revelation: that the knots themselves have become the language *of my art*. Every new knot I learn is like learning another letter in an alphabet. Alphabets and letters form words. Words communicate. So the knots are my new means of communication. They are my language. They are my voice.

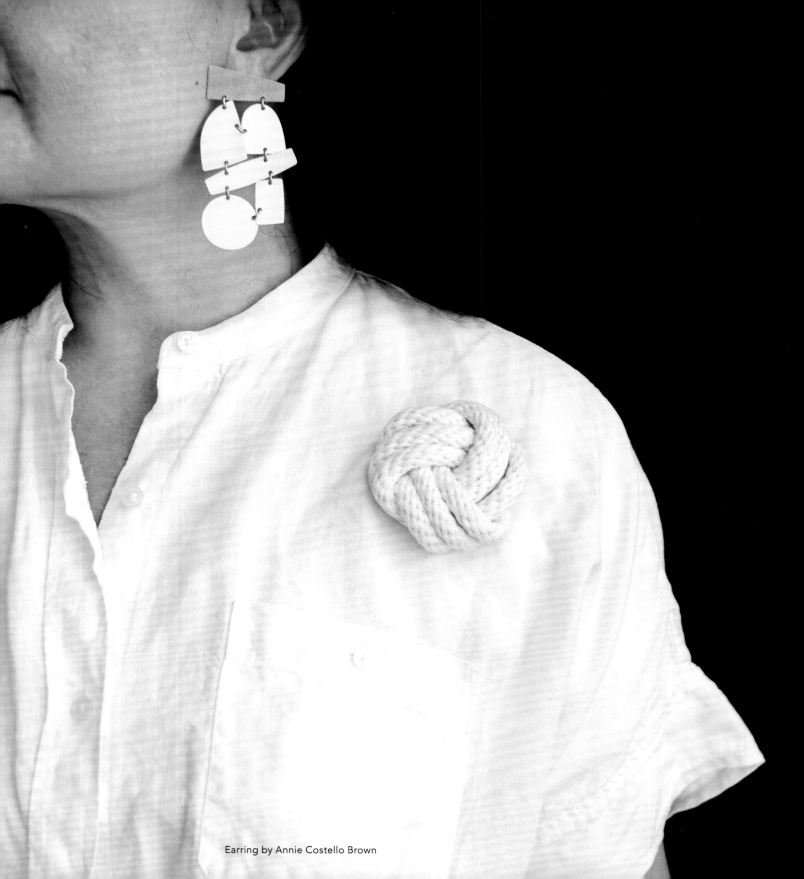

Earring by Annie Costello Brown

tripled trefoil / tweenie

This knot has so many talking points packed into it that one almost forgets how pretty it is.

For example, given how it looks, you might be surprised to learn the Tripled Trefoil starts out as the humble Overhand Knot, that building block form known to all of us (page 22). When the Overhand Knot's ends are joined, it is considered a Trefoil, which is known by mathematicians as the simplest form of "non-trivial knot."

Mathematical knot theory is a fascinating field with which I have only the most basic familiarity. Briefly, mathematical knots are concerned with topology, or the study of deformations in abstract space. Mathematical knots are closed loops and, hence, lack ends; instead, the knot runs along a continuous line. One way mathematicians classify knots is by the number of crossings they display. The Trefoil Knot has the fewest possible crossings— three—and cannot be simplified to fewer than three crossings; therefore, our mathematicians would also deem it a "prime knot."

With its ends overlapped, the single-stranded Trefoil can be drawn taut into a handsome triangular stopper knot, which Clifford Ashley called the "Tweenie." Even better, if left flat, then doubled or tripled where the cord runs parallel to the original line, it makes a handsome flat knot, and one might stop there. But best of all, if drawn up carefully into a pillowy sphere, we can say the resulting knot shares qualities with the Monkey's Fist Knot—namely, that it exhibits multiple interlocking rings and can act as a knot covering around an object.

I'm so in love with this cool knot that I trim the legs to wear it as a brooch.

MATERIALS

5' (1.5 m) of ⁵⁄₁₆" (7.5-mm) cotton braid

Corkboard and pins (optional)

Hinged pin backing (optional)

Needle and thread or your choice of glue (optional)

1. On a tabletop, lay out a loose, open Overhand Knot as shown, with the working end exiting behind the knot.

2. Place the ends near each other. Note that if you were to join these ends, you'd have the mathematical Trefoil Knot, albeit one with a very large lower lobe.

   Prepare to draw the working end into the knot, running parallel to the original line.

3. Lead the working end along the inside of the original line. This is called doubling.

   Continue leading the cord through the knot, following the original line. Do not twist the parallel lines. Keep them flat, like a ribbon.

   If your rope isn't cooperating and the knot's three lobes do not stay distinct from each other, it can help to pin the knot to a corkboard. Three or four pins should be sufficient.

4. You can triple, or even quadruple, the line. Here, I'm beginning the tripling pass.

   When you've completed the desired number of passes, gradually work out the slack, so the three lobes are of equal size and shape and there are no gaps. This must be done bit by bit, so it will take a while.

   If you pinned the knot to a corkboard, remove (or occasionally change the locations of) the pins while working the knot snug.

5 The **Tripled** *Flat* **Trefoil**. Isn't it gorgeous?

You could stop here, trim both ends, tuck the left end under the knot's left lobe, and use as a flat mat or coaster.

6 If you want to take the knot to the next stage, carefully pick it up and nestle your fingers in the center of its back side.

Let the perimeter of the knot drape down around your fingers, like raw pizza dough.

Continue tightening the knot. Because its next overall shape is not flat but more like a rounded cushion, there will be quite a bit more slack to work out. It takes *forever*.

7 When the knot reaches its final shape, a tripled triangular face, as shown here, is visible on the front of the knot, and another similar face is visible on back.

The knot should hold its compact shape when you let it go. If it does not hold its shape, you haven't worked it snug enough.

Press the knot flat with the palm of your hand to coax it into a cushioned disk shape.

Trim the ends and tuck them, then you can sew or glue on a pin back. Similarly, you can sew or glue the trimmed ends in place, if desired.

cowboy's pretzel flat knot

In the world of knotting, flat knots are a category unto themselves. As mats, they are staples of nautical decor and indeed have a performance function as well, preventing chafing and providing foothold on deck. Rendered at a smaller scale, they provide distinguished embellishment to military uniforms. As the Year of Knots progressed, I came to understand that many knots have both a flat and a "drawn together" state. The Chinese Button (page 75) is a classic example of this: I would be hard-pressed to name a favorite between its spherical button state and its gorgeous, symmetrical flattened state.

The shape of the Cowboy's Pretzel is another of the mathematician's simple "prime knots," a closed loop displaying, in the Pretzel's case, four crossings that cannot be reduced to fewer crossings. Fun fact: Cowboys reportedly use it for a lariat trick, because with a single flick, the knot turns from a pretzel to a figure 8.

As if all that wasn't interesting enough, I noticed that there is a difference between the single-strand version of this knot, which can be quadrupled by leading the one working cord four times alongside the original line, and a *four*-strand version of the knot, where the knot is made just once, working four *separate* strands *simultaneously*. This Four-Strand Cowboy's Pretzel, while so simple to make, features eight beautiful ends begging to be seized together and left long for added drama as a wall hanging.

In this tutorial, I'll demonstrate making the single-strand, Quadrupled Single-Strand Cowboy's Pretzel pictured on page 126. And I'd highly recommend you whip up its cousin, the Four-Strand Cowboy's Pretzel, pictured on this page with its extravagantly long ends and decorative gold seizing.

MATERIALS

For the Quadrupled Single-Strand Cowboy's Pretzel:

15' (4.6 m) of ⁵⁄₁₆" (7.5-mm) cotton braid

For the Four-Strand Cowboy's Pretzel:

Four 10' (3-m) strands of ⁵⁄₁₆" (7.5-mm) cotton braid

Embroidery thread or other "small stuff" (optional; see page 17)

KNOTS

COWBOY'S PRETZEL

SEIZING WITH RACKING TURNS (optional; see page 114)

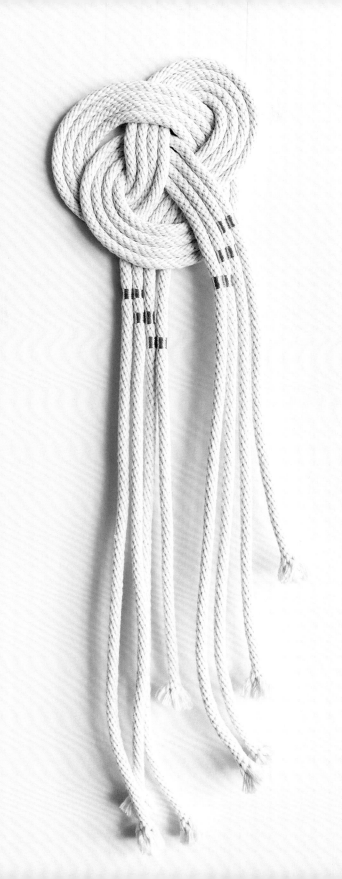

WORKING END

1 Lay the working cord over its standing end to form a single loop.

2 Draw the working end through the loop to form a second loop. Ensure the crossings are as shown. They must alternate *over* and *under* throughout the line's journey.

3 Lay the working end along the inside of (below) the original line.

   Draw the working end up into the knot and pull through so the bottom lobe of the pretzel is the same size as the left and right lobes.

   To make the Quadrupled Single-Strand Cowboy's Pretzel, continue to the next page.

   To make the **Four-Strand Cowboy's Pretzel**, see step 4 on page 127.

4 Draw the working end through the knot, following parallel to the original pretzel line and never crossing it.

   Continue passing the cord through the knot until you have four lines tracing the knot.

5 When the four passes are complete, it will take considerable working to even out the lobe sizes and shrink any visible gaps.

It's so beautiful!

6 I find this part of the process—smoothing out the four-strand "ribbon" and eliminating gaps—very soothing and satisfying.

Trim the ends so they're not visible.

(Continued from page 126)

4 To make the **Four-Strand Cowboy's Pretzel**, simply repeat the closed pretzel shape on previous page with a second strand, laying it alongside the original.

Repeat with the third and fourth cords, then adjust the knot so it is snug and no gaps show.

You can also make the pretzel in a single go by working the four separate strands *simultaneously*, taking care to keep the strands from crossing over each other.

Before adding the seizing, it's best to first hold the knot against the wall, rotating it in order to determine your favorite orientation and ensuring the legs hang smoothly, like flat ribbons.

Trim the legs to the length desired and seize together with small stuff in a decorative pattern, if you like (see page 114).

the squid

In the Year of Knots, I included two knots named after animals: the Dragonfly and the Caterpillar. Clifford Ashley greatly admired Chinese and Japanese decorative knotting, and after making the Caterpillar and the Dragonfly, I too caught the bug (ahem). Many of these decorative knots, especially Chinese priest cords and lantern cords, are made by simply knotting a pair of strands in a vertical and symmetrical fashion incorporating many—even dozens of—individual knots in their construction.

Simple variations on square knots and over-under crossings can yield an infinite number of patterns. Although the point of this book is to encourage you to go *beyond* the basic three or four knots that appear in macramé, there's nothing wrong with riffing on those elementary knots to find your own combinations. It's like being a musician: First you play other people's songs, but when you've mastered the basics, you write your own.

The Squid appeared one day as I was playing with the possibilities inherent in repeated square knots arranged in different combos and peppered with over-under crossings.

In the flow of making, I focused on proportion—the width of the piece versus the rope diameter—and I knotted without a preconceived notion of the final shape. Making representational work isn't my thing, but how could I *not* name this one the Squid?

MATERIALS
**Two 5' (1.5-m) strands of ⁵⁄₁₆"
(7.5-mm) cotton braid**

KNOTS
SQUARE KNOT
(page 42)

SINGLE HITCH
(page 82)

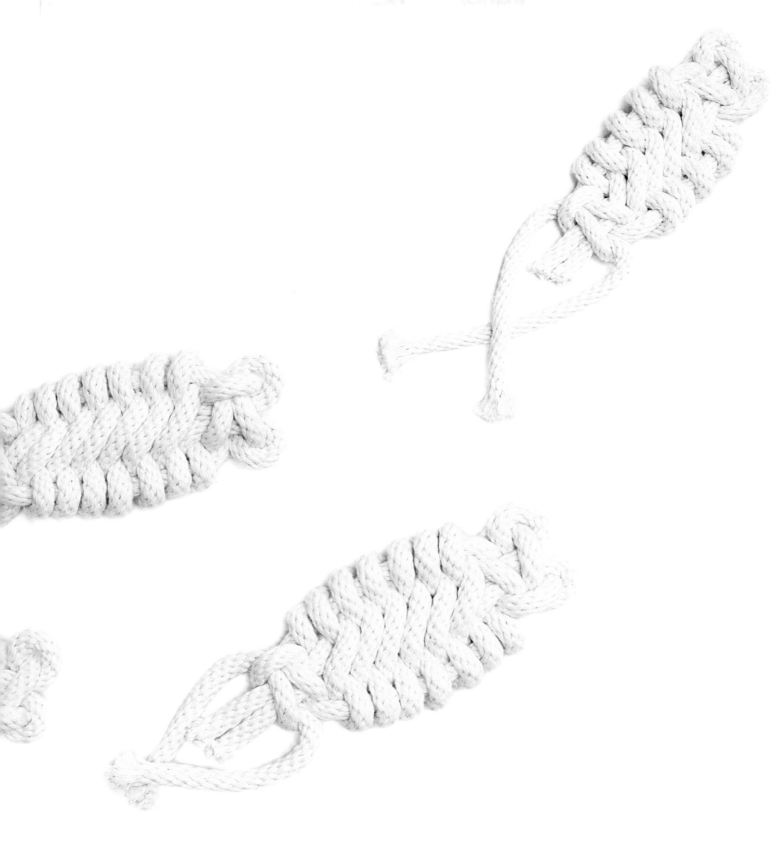

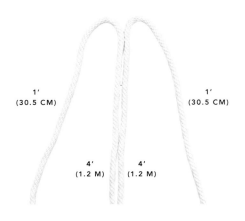

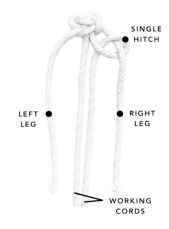

SINGLE HITCH

LEFT LEG

RIGHT LEG

WORKING CORDS

1 Divide each cord into a 1' (30.5-cm) part and a 4' (1.2-m) part.

Arrange the pair of cords as mirror images, as shown, with the 1' (30.5-cm) parts on the outside and the 4' (1.2-m) parts on the inside.

2 Using the short outer cords, tie a Square Knot around the center long pair.

As you already know, a Square Knot is two Half Knots, one left and one right.

This is the squid's head.

3 The two long inner cords now become the working cords.

Make a Single Hitch around the right leg. In other words: Draw the right working cord behind the right leg, then around in front of it and downward behind the working cord itself, creating a little loop.

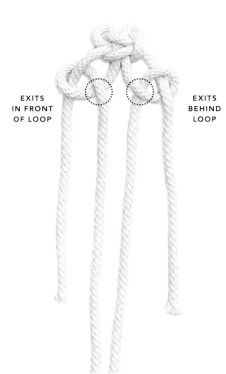

EXITS IN FRONT OF LOOP

EXITS BEHIND LOOP

4 Draw the left working cord in front of the left leg, then around the back of it and downward in front of the working cord itself, forming another Single Hitch.

Note that this hitch is slightly different from the first hitch you just made. It is not a mirror image. The first exits in back; the second exits in front. Look at your knot and make sure the hitches are doing this.

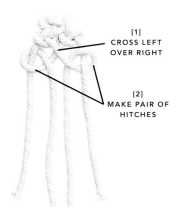

[1]
CROSS LEFT
OVER RIGHT

[2]
MAKE PAIR OF
HITCHES

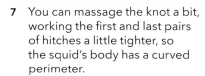

5 Now that you've tied the first pair of hitches, draw them snug.

Cross the left working cord *over* the right working cord, trading places, then make another pair of hitches, exactly the same as the first pair.

In other words, crossing the working cords means the left working cord will now hitch over the right leg, and the right working cord will hitch around the left leg.

Continue working down the legs of the knot using the same pattern: [1] cross left working cord over right, then [2] tie pair of Single Hitches.

Tighten the hitches as you go.

6 Repeat until you have seven pairs of hitches.

The vertical column of diagonal crossings between the hitches should be uniform and parallel.

7 You can massage the knot a bit, working the first and last pairs of hitches a little tighter, so the squid's body has a curved perimeter.

Using the short outer legs, tie a Square Knot around the longer inner cords.

8 Trim the long working cords.

sharing

During this whole process of making and learning the knots, which I would describe as *inward*, I was also pushing my work *outward*. Because when I started prioritizing my own creativity, I was on my third career. I didn't necessarily feel late to the party, but from a practical standpoint, it was clear that I had no time to waste. Unlike many of my artist and musician friends who started in their twenties, I hadn't been sharing my work for decades, so I cultivated opportunities to expose it to an audience. Here's what I did.

An integral part of the Year of Knots was sharing images of it, something I recommend you do as well, because it serves the dual purpose of both keeping you honest and getting the work out into the world. I've always loved watching other artists' creative process, so I figured folks would be interested in mine, as well. Those were the first reasons I started posting to social media, but I didn't anticipate all the ways in which "putting myself out there" would pay off. I credit that effort with so much of what I have achieved today.

Think about it: If I had simply completed the Year of Knots in solitude and then hoped to get noticed *afterward*, it wouldn't have been as fresh and immediate, and, frankly, it would

have been a one-off story. **By inviting the audience into my process and documenting it daily, I had the opportunity to be in conversation with others for the whole year.** Some artists work in obscurity and privacy, and then put the work out there when it's done. Not me. If I shared it only at the end, the process would have been lost. By posting the knots every day, it became *about* the process.

The work unfolded in real time, and indeed, it found its form that way. Since I hadn't set out to make a single composite piece, but many small knots, the slow realization that it *was* a single artwork emerged from the work *as* it was being created. **Look at your own journey of and to creativity—how you got here, what you do with what you've learned—and recognize that growth as part of what makes your work rich.** For me, growth—not just in the number of knots but also of the accumulation of knowledge—became another layer of *meaning*, in that while the idea for the Year of Knots sprang forth fully formed, the execution of it had to be done incrementally, on a daily basis. To manifest it took a year.

If the work was about unfolding itself, the process was about story. I believe we all enjoy watching ourselves and others transform, because everyone wants that. When you're not growing, you're stagnant. That's not living.

So, sharing your story is one of the most authentic things you can do. Chronicling what I was making was an honest way to figure out who I was becoming. It was a story about a person who, at the beginning of the year, didn't know what it meant to be an artist, if I was allowed to be one, how to do it, how to articulate it, and, most importantly, how to own it. Yet, by the end of the project, I could confidently identify as an artist without feeling like an imposter. I grew.

So the social media account was my daily journal of the work process. But it was also serving a bigger purpose in terms of my career and everything that would come afterward. It wasn't just garnering fans and likes; it was planting seeds and building a platform for new kinds of work: gallery offers, immersive installations, collaborations with interior designers and architects, and even a book deal. Much of that came about because I shared my work. And just think about the magnificence of that. It's free. It's something you can do every day. And if you commit to it, you can attract all kinds of professional attention and even make a new career for yourself.

Isn't the internet an amazing means by which we find our people? It is how I connected with the mighty men of the YouTube paracord world, the fearless female macramé makers, the seaworthy sailors of all stripes, and the International Guild of Knot Tyers and its old-fashioned chat rooms. They found me and I found them.

Another way I found to put my work out there was through public speaking. This was a huge step for me because all my life I'd been afraid of getting on a stage. But when I got the first invitation to do so, I accepted. At that moment, I was halfway through the Year of Knots and had never summed up my life into a TED Talk format. Believe me, there were tears

and all-nighters. But I'm so glad I forced myself to do it. By distilling what I was doing into a narrative, I authored my story. I was already living it, but this forced me to reflect on it and find meaning within it.

So I spoke at a design conference for the Apple community, to SECA (Society for the Encouragement of Contemporary Art, an SFMOMA group who underwrite a prestigious biennial art award), and to professional creatives at design firms and advertising agencies. And wow: Responses ranged from audience members with tears in their eyes to people telling me I had inspired them to quit their day jobs to pursue their passions. Such positive feedback buoyed me.

It sounds daunting to narrate your own story, **but really, all you have to do is tell the truth. I think every person's story is fascinating and deserves to be told.** As I said, we all want to transform, so I consider it part of my practice to share the story (hence this book).

Other artists will tell you it's just about the work and not to bring their story into it. Not me. I'm about the journey. And that's literally manifested in my work because my *lines* take a journey, starting in one place, looping around and ending up transformed. So, I accepted all the invitations, which forced me to not only speak in public, but to push my work forward. By framing my story as a journey, it opened up new ways for me to think about the concept of the line, and that, in turn, made the work evolve.

At the same time, I started wondering how to get the work in front of magazine editors. One day, as we were knotting Helix Lights, my friend Hannah, an accomplished musician and filmmaker, asked me why I hadn't hired a PR person. Um, because I had always thought public relations was something restricted to big brands or celebrities—i.e., it was *not* punk. My old-school DIY sensibility never thought to ask for help. But Hannah confided that she always hires a PR team when she releases a new album. It suddenly made sense for me to hire an expert to do something I didn't have time or skills to cover. And so I did. I found a press rep who not only understood my work but wanted to champion it, and that was a great move. Within what felt like weeks, the *San Francisco Chronicle* did a Sunday-issue piece on me, which resulted in one of my first art patrons finding me. This was a seminal moment because it showed me a lesson I'd see recur again and again: **Every time you get a piece of press, it causes a chain reaction that brings fresh interest and opportunities.** It advances the work and the possibilities with every story.

Initially, people had wanted to purchase a product from me—say, a small wall hanging or a single light—but with this article and other pieces around that time, my work was being shown in a new way, and suddenly people weren't just looking to have a single commodity, but wanted my eye to envision a space from scratch and my hands to create something custom. That was the beginning of my main clientele shifting from lifestyle shoppers to professional designers and fine-art collectors, which changed the game from one-off sales to large commissions and consulting. Obviously, that's a different sort of fee structure, so it propelled me forward yet again. This was a subtle shift, but a huge one in terms of the transition from craft maker to place maker. **The lesson I learned was that press coverage can help bring about the type of work you want to do by reaching the customers who will support you in doing it.**

So over the course of the year, I had this multipronged manner of putting myself out there, from social media to speaking engage-ments to press. It was all going well, the work was evolving, as was I . . . Things were peachy. But then something really big happened. *Wired* called.

A *Wired* design editor had noticed my work and reached out about doing a feature. It was January 2017, right at the tail end of the Year of Knots, and it felt as though she must have waited for me to see it through, and then pounced on the story. I was over the moon that a publication—or anyone "important"—saw it as a single, whole piece, not just a daily practice, and talked about it in terms that expressed what a big achievement it was. They also didn't feel the need to cover my products or other work. They believed that the Year of Knots stood on its own merit and deserved attention all by itself. And it started catching. In short order, three or four other key press entities with huge readerships (including Martha Stewart) followed suit with their own articles and I was now operating in a new dimension.

How do I know? Because a short while later, Facebook called and invited me to be a participant in their Facebook Artist in Residence (AIR) program. Can you imagine how thrilled I was? When you go to Facebook's campus, there's art everywhere. Wrapped around corners, climbing up stairwells, suspended from ceilings. Every available surface has art, and this is true of all of their campuses worldwide. We talked about what the residency piece would look like, and from among the options I proposed, they decided on an edition of the Year of Knots (because, of course, I can never part with the original). So there was the wonderful good feeling of knowing both that I was being properly compensated for a work that took a year to conceive and execute, and also that the work was going to a loving home where it would be seen and appreciated.

sharing

heaving line knot and dune creature

In order to get rope from ship to shore, you tie a heavy, dense Heaving Line Knot at one end of a line in order to make it throw-able. The classic Monkey's Fist Knot is a type of Heaving Line Knot, and the Doughnut (page 60) can also be used this way. Most knots from this family aren't necessarily made with an eye to aesthetics, but Clifford Ashley, as much of an aesthete as he was a historian and knot junkie, invented this stunning version. Since I'm constantly on the lookout for the beauty in the functional, it should come as no surprise that I fell in love with this Heaving Line Knot.

In fact, the first time I tied the knot, I didn't want to stop. I played with elongating the length, experimenting with thicker rope, and varying the ways I tightened the legs, which caused the long knot to curve. And just like that, it came alive. I christened it the Dune Creature after the sandworm in the eponymous film. (For fun, I invite you to google "Dune Giger worm.")

I tend to make the Heaving Line Knot either short and cute (like the one in this tutorial) or elongated into the Dune Creature.

MATERIALS

4' (1.2 m) of ⁵⁄₁₆" (7.5-mm) cotton braid

Bent-nose pliers

"Small stuff" of your choice (see page 17), such as embroidery thread or satin cord (optional)

Needle (optional)

My rule of thumb is that the knot requires about twenty times the desired final length (not including "tail"). In the tutorial, I'm using 4' (1.2 m) of rope, or 48" (120 cm), which results in a 2½" (6.5-cm) Heaving Line Knot.

KNOTS

HEAVING LINE KNOT

SEIZING WITH RACKING TURNS (page 114)

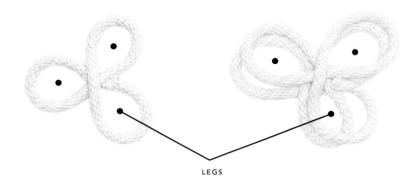

LEGS

　Before starting the knot, familiarize yourself with its general structure.

Like the Multiple Figure 8 Knot (page 28), the Heaving Line Knot consists of core cords wrapped with racking turns. But while the Multiple Figure 8 features turns wrapped around two legs in a figure 8 style, here they wrap around *three* legs to form a shamrock, or three-leaf clover, shape.

The rope will always travel around a leg, then return to the center and head toward the next leg, and so on.

The shamrock will simply repeat itself in layers until the desired knot length has been reached.

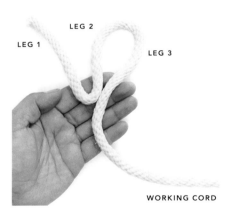

LEG 2
LEG 1
LEG 3

WORKING CORD

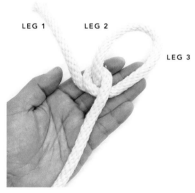

LEG 1　LEG 2

LEG 3

2　Arrange one end of the rope into three legs, as shown. The legs are the core cords around which the shamrocks will be wrapped.

As you work, do not allow yourself to become confused by the fact that the three legs are connected. Think of them as three separate legs.

3　Draw the working cord around the base of leg 2, circling left to right behind the leg, then forward through the loop formed by legs 2 and 3.

This turn is the first third of the shamrock.

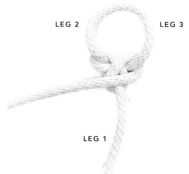

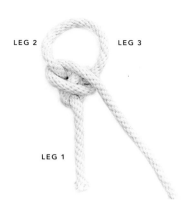

4 You will want to adjust leg 1's position so that it is equidistant from legs 2 and 3. In effect, each leg is a point at the corners of an equilateral triangle.

Therefore, in the photo, I've moved leg 1 closer to leg 3 and am pointing it downward. But, note that when you are holding the knot in your hand, you'll want to point leg 1 *up*, the same way legs 2 and 3 are pointing up.

Now make a second turn around leg 1, moving right to left behind it.

End this step by drawing the working cord *between* the other two legs, crossing over the top of the first loop you made.

5 Complete the first full shamrock by turning the working cord around leg 3. The cord is already to the left of leg 3, so the move is simply to draw the cord behind leg 3 and then forward.

Finish by drawing the cord between the other two legs (1 and 2) and working out any slack in the shamrock.

6 Continue stacking two or three more shamrocks on top of each other all the way up the legs. Remember that each lobe of the shamrock consists of [1] turning the working cord once *around* a leg and then [2] drawing it *between* the other two legs.

The photo above shows the first turn in the new shamrock. The working cord turns once around leg 2, then comes to rest between the other two legs (1 and 3).

CONNECTED LEGS

SINGLE LEG

NO SLACK AT TAIL

NO SLACK AT HEAD

7 As you work, make the turns snug. You will have the opportunity to properly tighten them later, but it's best to make them snug at the get-go. Otherwise, the knot may become so loose that you get confused.

8 When you are almost done knotting, the legs will be short, so it's important that you have developed an understanding of which is which. At this point, you can forget about the numbers and just think of them as the two legs that are connected and the single leg.

When the knot is the length desired, the last turn should be the one that goes *between* the connected legs, toward the center, and comes to rest touching the single leg.

If you've ended the shamrock correctly, both the working end and the single leg should meet. Together they form a "tail."

If your last turn causes the two ends to splay, you didn't finish with the correct turn. Either undo or add turns in order to finish as described above. The photo shows the correct last turn.

9 To finish the knot, firmly tug on the three leg cords in such a way that the shamrock layers get smooshed together and the slack from all three of the legs is released out at the single leg. There's a certain order to tugging the three legs that you will figure out. You want there to be no "leg slack" at the tail or at the head of the knot.

Additionally, there must be no leg cords showing *between* the shamrock layers. The shamrock layers should be smushed against each other, like the examples on the next page.

Finally, work the slack out of each of the shamrock "petals" one by one with the bent-nose pliers. Start at the head and work *toward* the tail. You have to do them in this certain order and rotate the knot a lot, which will become obvious as you do it. You want the petals to feel snug against the leg cords.

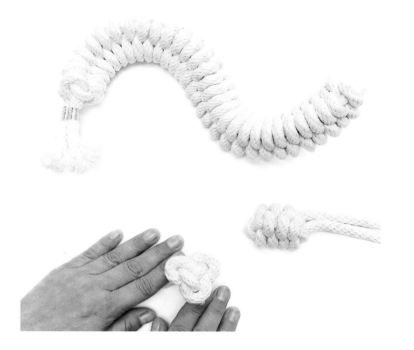

10 Trim the two ends to form a cute tail.

If desired, seize the tail cords together with small stuff and a needle, using the multiple racking turns from page 114.

11 To make my Dune Creature, increase the target length of the Heaving Line Knot to at least 1′ (30.5 cm)—which means starting with 20′ (6.1 m) of rope!

Then, when you reach the step where you are working the slack out of the legs (page 140), it becomes a matter of creatively tightening the legs in certain spots so that the knot curves. In other words, you can tug at the legs not only from their ends, but also by plunging the bent-nose pliers into the middles of the legs. There's no straightforward way to instruct this. You have to do it by feel. It's a magical moment!

put it
out there

Treating your creativity seriously means giving it every chance to succeed. Not having a plan to get the work "out there" is self-sabotaging. So if you are hoping to sell your work or make it into a career, be smart and be practical. You can do this in several ways.

SHARE YOUR WORK. Even better: the work in progress. It is the only way to know if it's resonating with anyone other than yourself. Making your process and progress visible will forge a genuine connection with your audience, who will feel as if they are there alongside you as you move through the project *together*. When you learn out in the open, viewers respond.

And don't worry about perfection: people love to follow along and watch you grow.

CULTIVATE SOCIAL MEDIA. Embrace technology's ability to connect you with an audience. I regarded this task as (a very pleasant) part of my job: posting consistently at the same time each day, adopting the tone of a friendly expert reporting from the front lines, answering comments, and thanking by name those folks kind enough to leave a compliment.

ACCEPT EVERY INVITATION TO SPEAK ABOUT YOUR WORK. And tell your story honestly and openly. Don't try to be someone you aren't. You are enough as is. Nervous? As advertising legend and rollicking feminist Cindy Gallop points out, "Fear of what other people will think is the single most paralyzing dynamic in business and in life." Stop caring what other people think. Try speaking to the tiniest, most welcoming audience first. Do it publicly a few times and I promise you'll not only get over being nervous, you'll discover the wonderful feeling that comes from telling your story.

AMPLIFY YOUR REACH. Give yourself the opportunity for your good work to be seen widely. This might take the form of adding a publicist to your team, or it might mean learning about how the press/publications world works, and doing it yourself.

After spending so much time at Apple—with its near-flawless approach to marketing, advertising, and the voice with which it speaks to customers—and also working with startup independent app developers, I've come to believe that an outreach plan is nonnegotiable when starting a new business or career. And this absolutely applies to the art and craft world. PR help is not "buying" press or cheating, as I had worried. It focuses your audience-building efforts toward folks who can amplify your voice: editors. I had neither the time nor the inclination to build up the relationships of trust with the editorial teams at the publications who I *knew* would like my work, if they only had the opportunity to see it, so I hired experts who could do this properly. This is one of the best investments I've ever made.

Your future customers read these magazines, and this is how they will find you.

If you're bootstrapping your own plan, it's OK to start small, with podcasters and small publications who are at the same level you are and will welcome an articulate artist to their platform. You can build a community of like-minded art and craft appreciators in this way. And you can keep this community—along with your customers and clients—informed via a regular email newsletter.

WHERE APPROPRIATE, HIRE A PROFESSIONAL PHOTOGRAPHER. Sure, I shot the daily Year of Knots photos with my iPhone and happily mastered photo-editing apps along the way, but I asked my photographer friends for tips on how to make the shots sing. And for *all* of the larger installations I do today, I invest in pros, because professional photographers are worth their weight in gold. They see the work with fresh eyes. They help you put your best foot forward to the world. They'll supply you with both web- and print-ready shots at a high quality you don't need to learn to achieve yourself. This way, you will be prepared for your work to be shown in magazines, newspapers, and online. And for publications with small-to-nonexistent budgets for photography, you'll be helping them by supplying beautiful imagery, and in turn, they'll be more receptive to presenting your work in their pages.

captain hardy's eye splice

I first saw Captain Hardy's Eye Splice in a photo of an old-fashioned knot board on display at the New Bedford Whaling Museum in Massachusetts. Having already learned all of the other knots on the board, I was immediately drawn to the one unknown. Recently, I saw the same knot in a slim handbook, where it is identified as the Cat's Paw Eye Splice (see the three-part claws?).

It's amazing to me that today I can encounter a knot and successfully decode its construction, but that's what a year of daily study will do. Immediately, I made the splice.

This elegant knot is a good place to enter the world of splicing because it's not complicated, and in the process of making it you will get comfortable with opening and manipulating twisted, multistrand rope.

MATERIALS

3' (91 cm) of 1" (2.5-cm) three-strand cotton rope

Paper tape or electrical tape

Fid (optional—you won't need it with cotton rope, but stiffer rope fibers such as manila are more easily opened with the tool)

Bent-nose pliers

"Small stuff" for Common Whipping (see pages 17, 19)

KNOTS

CAPTAIN HARDY'S EYE SPLICE

COMMON WHIPPING (page 28)

Stranded rope wants to unravel, so prevent this with a good amount of tape, enough to cover at least 1" (2.5 cm) of the rope end and to form a tapered tip extending out from the end of the rope.

Tip: Always pull a longer piece of tape than you think you need . . . and it will likely be the right amount. This is some sort of law of nature.

1 Choose a point about 1' (30.5 cm) from the end of the rope. Grasp a strand and pull it toward the right, away from its sisters.

With cotton rope, this should be easy enough to do with your fingers. If you're using manila rope or something similarly stiff, a fid may be helpful.

At first, especially with very thick rope, it will seem as if the strands aren't *meant* to be separated, and they will resist. Persevere. It may feel weird, but the strands will open.

LITTLE LOOP

2 Rotate the freed, right strand counterclockwise, to the left. If this is confusing, rotate the strand to and fro in both directions. The direction that it *wants* to go in is the right one; there'll be less resistance.

3 Insert the tip of the other rope leg upward through the free strand's little loop, heading away from the eye and toward the rope end.

4 Pull the inserted leg all the way through until the eye is the size desired.

I find it's easy to pull with my fingers, but bent-nose pliers may be helpful to grasp the taped end.

5 Free the next strand above the one just worked, moving toward the tail and away from the eye.

Repeat until you have three spliced loops, each time freeing a strand, rotating it counterclockwise, and inserting the other leg up through the little loop.

6 Flip the whole thing over horizontally and repeat the same three tucks on the other leg of the knot.

7 Whip the ends (page 28), then trim off the tape.

At first, I was so knocked out by the gorgeousness of Captain Hardy's Eye Splice that I assumed it is merely decorative. But, after making it, I observed its strength and security. As long as the whipping holds, there's no way for the splice to move.

eye splice

I used to find splices intimidating, and I studiously avoided them for a full two months during the Year of Knots. But splices are also fascinating and so beautiful. Just the concept of things coming apart in order to join themselves back together: There's a lot of scope for the imagination. Splices join two lines, or form eyes, or loops, in a single line. And many splices are known to be stronger and more secure than the rope from which they are made, meaning that under force, the rope would fail before the splice would. Finally, the jargon used to describe the splice-making process—such as *crotch*, *cuntline*, *heart yarns*, *dog's cock*, *marriage*, etc.—is as colorful as it is clarifying.

I needed to learn to splice. In a sense, so much of the Year of Knots was about facing my fears head-on and working through them.

To splice, you separate the strands of twisted rope in order to interweave other strands. All splices have this in common, and differ in such aspects as the number and configuration of tucks, with variations introduced for joining ropes of unequal quantities of strands, interweaving other materials (such as wire), and splicing shapes. One wonderful splice is called Dog Pointing. It is a way to turn the ends of strands back into their own rope end, for a clean finish.

If you've already made Captain Hardy's Eye Splice (page 146), then you are comfortable with opening strands in the bight of a rope. Here, with the Eye Splice, I introduce the concept of multiple tucks.

MATERIALS

3' (91 cm) of 1" (2.5-cm) right-laid cotton rope

Paper tape or electrical tape

Fid (optional—you won't need it with cotton rope, but stiffer materials such as manila are more easily opened with the tool)

Bent-nose pliers

In this tutorial, I'm using 3' (91 cm) of 1" (2.5-cm) right-laid cotton rope. Learning to splice benefits from using large-diameter rope as it's easier to see what you are doing, but you can use a thinner variety, in which case less than three feet of length will be sufficient.

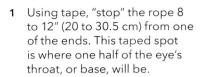

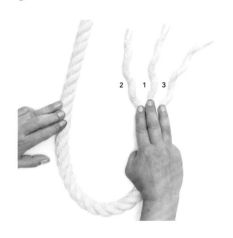

1 Using tape, "stop" the rope 8 to 12" (20 to 30.5 cm) from one of the ends. This taped spot is where one half of the eye's throat, or base, will be.

2 Unfurl the three strands and tape their ends to prevent fraying.

As you handle them, the strands will naturally lose some of their twist, which is normal. The twists will be restored in the process of making the splice.

3 Separate the three strands and notice how I've labeled them. It's not important what we call them, so I've simply assigned them numbers for the order in which they will move.

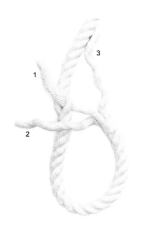

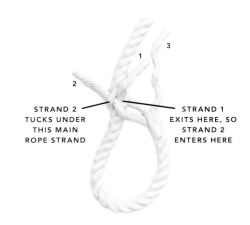

STRAND 2
TUCKS UNDER
THIS MAIN
ROPE STRAND

STRAND 1
EXITS HERE, SO
STRAND 2
ENTERS HERE

4 On the body of the rope, decide where you want the eye's throat (or base) to be, and open the strands there, pulling one strand to the right.

In my example, I've opened the rope about 14″ (35.5 cm) away from the taped stop, so the eye will have a circumference of that length.

For learning purposes, it is not important how big the finished eye is, as long as it is not so small that you run out of room to work.

5 Do not twist the opened strand into a loop, as you did in Captain Hardy's Eye Splice. Just hold the rope open.

Draw strand 1 (the middle strand) under the open rope strand, entering from behind on the right and exiting from the left. Pull strand 1 partway through, but not all the way yet.

6 Now pick up strand 2.

Position the tip of the strand 2 at the point where strand 1 is *exiting*. Notice the main rope strand immediately to the left. Tuck strand 2 under it.

In other words, where the middle strand exits is where the left strand enters. The left strand tucks under the strand to its left.

Again, pull the strand only partway through.

STRAND 1
HAS ALREADY
ENTERED HERE, SO
STRAND 3 WILL
EXIT HERE

3

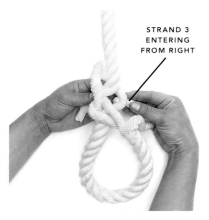

STRAND 3
ENTERING
FROM RIGHT

7 Rotate the splice slightly left to reveal the right side of the splice, where the next step takes place.

Look closely at where strand 1 *enters* the splice. This is where you want strand 3 to *exit* from.

Position strand 3 to the right of the entire splice.

8 If it isn't already, pry open the main rope to the right of strand 1.

Tuck strand 3 leftward under the opened, rightmost strand of the main rope. In other words, where strand 1 enters is where strand 3 *exits*.

9 Pull all three strands firmly all the way through, so the taped stop meets the splice.

Twist each strand gently to restore its twist structure. While doing so, you'll notice that the strands move through the tucks a bit morev and feel as if they're settling into place. It is a very satisfying feeling!

Turn the splice over in your hand, examining it from all angles. If you've made it correctly, you'll notice that the tucked strands are equidistant, each separated from each other by one strand from the main body of the rope.

Phew, you've survived the first round of tucks. The Eye Splice will be tucked twice more.

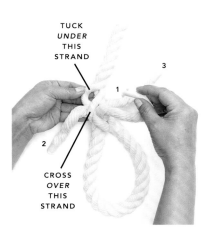

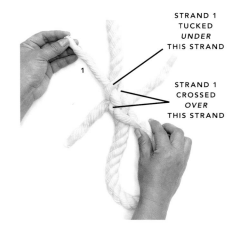

TUCK *UNDER* THIS STRAND

CROSS *OVER* THIS STRAND

STRAND 1 TUCKED *UNDER* THIS STRAND

STRAND 1 CROSSED *OVER* THIS STRAND

10 Tuck each of the three strands leftward *over* one main body strand and *under* one main body strand. If this already makes sense, go ahead and do it, or follow these detailed steps:

Grasp strand 1 again. Let strands 2 and 3 fall out of the way toward the eye, so they don't get mistaken for strands from the main body of the rope.

Notice the two main body rope strands to the left of strand 1. Draw strand 1 leftward *over* the first and *under* the next.

11 Pull strand 1 all the way through.

12 Do the same with the remaining strands 2 and 3, always crossing leftward *over* its neighboring main body strand and tucking *under* the next main body strand.

Twist all three strands very tightly to help seat them into the splice.

13 Tuck all the strands a third time, exactly the way you made the second round of tucks.

Twist all the strands a final time to really seat them into the splice.

14 Three sets of tucks is probably sufficient for cotton rope, but if you're using particularly slippery synthetic fiber, add three more rounds of tucks.

Examine the splice. The tucks should be handsomely even, the strands should be twisted, and there should be no slack anywhere.

Trim the taped ends and remove the tape stop.

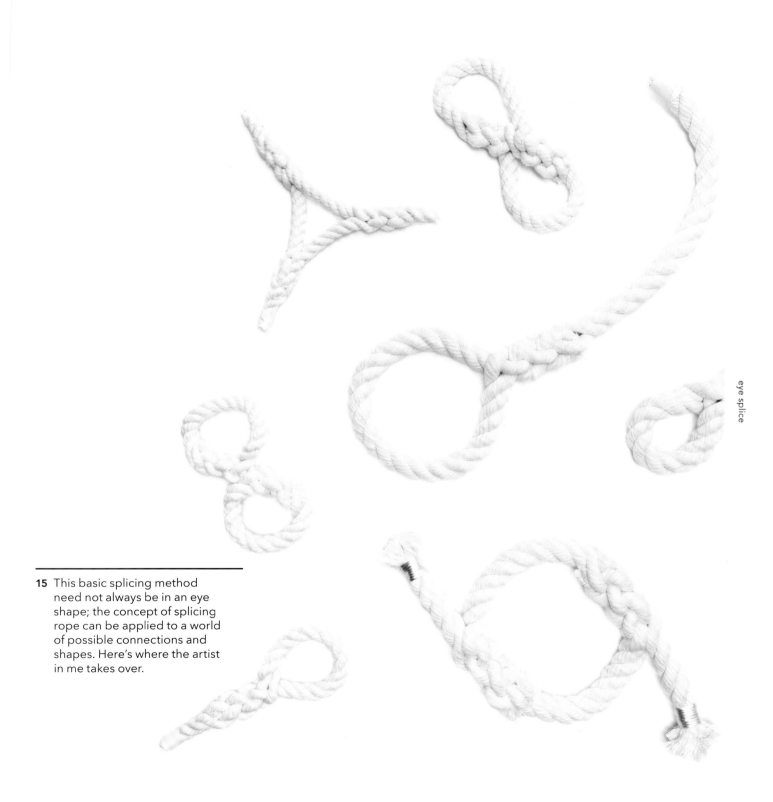

15 This basic splicing method
need not always be in an eye
shape; the concept of splicing
rope can be applied to a world
of possible connections and
shapes. Here's where the artist
in me takes over.

committing

**C**ommitment to your craft is an opportunity to visit the gamut of emotions on a daily basis: exhilaration, joy, gratitude . . . but also fear, insecurity, and doubt. My daily mindset swung like a pendulum, making each day feel different. On the best days, I buzzed with energy, filled with a happy curiosity about what each new knot would teach me and anticipating the sense of deep satisfaction learning each would bring.

But on a few bad days, I worried the Year of Knots was trivial, too simple, or self-indulgent. How dare I call it art? Sometimes a stray comment on social media reinforced my doubts. Other knotters (always male) found ways to tear the work down by scoffing at details, like frayed rope ends, while ignoring the larger point of the work.

A particularly frustrating day came with the Star Knot (page 160), a fiendishly complex type of button knot requiring dozens of steps that—for the life of me—I could not figure out how to make from its diagram. Finally, I reluctantly resorted to watching an online video tutorial and when I completed the Star Knot, I was filled with both the feeling of exhilaration (what an accomplishment!) and the feeling of being an imposter (I needed "extra help," damn it).

But I reminded myself that the only thing that mattered was my experience. I had framed the Year of Knots as a documentation of learning. Whenever I remembered that the objective was simply teaching myself something, it felt valid again. In other words, the meaning of the piece was more than just the knots themselves. It was the yearlong commitment, the daily act of making, the accumulation of learning, the attainment of fluency in a new language.

Each day is an opportunity to approach your work anew, and you get to choose the emotions with which to approach it. Be delighted by your emotions. You are living. When a bad day presents itself, identify it as such and you will retain the power: "Oh, hi there, bad day." When a piece doesn't turn out as well as you wanted it to, sit with what you learned (because you definitely learned something from the experience), then try again tomorrow.

On another hard day, I utterly failed to properly make an ambitious knot consisting of an ungainly seventy-two crossings. The knot was a terrible tangle, and after two hours of tying and retying, I gave up. I photographed and posted the mess anyway, feeling that there was a lesson in there somewhere. I could have made another knot to replace the tangle, but the fail felt *just as valuable*, because the tangle was saying something—about confusion and persistence, harmony and disharmony. And you know what? My commenters replied that they thought it was lovely anyway.

Now and then, tell the story of failure— and never forget your audience is rooting for you. **The story of your work is more than just a single day or an individual art piece.** What gives it resonance is the larger context of your journey. It's never about a single piece and whether it was "good" or "bad."

The first few months of the Year of Knots, I hewed closely to my "one knot a day" rule, and I'd feel like I was cheating if I needed a day off. But feeling guilty gets old quick. If life gets in the way, I say it's OK to make it easier on yourself while staying true to your commitment. And if I was feeling on a roll, obsessed with a single family of knots, I let myself make several in the same session. It didn't diminish the benefits of the daily practice.

After several months, I'd silenced all the negative voices in my head. My confidence was stable, even soaring. **You define the experience you want to have. By making your own rules, you'll set yourself up to succeed.**

multistrand star knot

Ah, the Multistrand Star Knot: the most difficult knot I learned during the Year of Knots. Having grown enamored with button knots, I attempted this in March, only three months into the project. I wasn't ready for it, and my knotting books' cryptic, jargon-heavy instructions confused more than they enlightened. After three or four attempts, frustrated and teary, I reluctantly resorted to YouTube. By my self-imposed standards for the Year of Knots, this felt like cheating. I wanted to learn from ye olde encyclopedias, the respected tomes written by experts who'd devoted their lives to knotting.

And yet, via YouTube, I fell happily headfirst into the world of para-cord. I love subcultures of all sorts, and this one comprises (mostly) men making (mostly) outdoor survival gear, such as knife sheaths, rifle straps, beer koozies, and complex Turk's Heads out of paracord, the thin, weatherproof nylon cord that comes in every color imaginable (including glow in the dark! Paracorders know how to party).

With your success in mind, I've broken down the process into bite-size steps that are as simple as I can make them. The most important concept to remember is that the same step is repeated once for *every* strand in the knot. Hence, because the Star in this tutorial has four strands, each step will be repeated four times, once for each strand in succession, before advancing to the next step.

I've made the Star Knot with as few as two cords, and three-, four-, and five-strand versions are shown on this page. Seven strands wasn't as pretty to me, but could be worth a try if your aesthetic runs in that direction.

MATERIALS

Four 3' (91-cm) strands of ⁵⁄₁₆" (7.5-mm) cotton braid

Rubber band

One 4' (1.2-m) length of ¼" (6-mm) cotton braid for Common Whipping (page 27), or more if using "small stuff" (see page 17)

KNOTS

MULTISTRAND STAR KNOT

COMMON WHIPPING

SKILLS

CROWNING AND TUCKING
(see page 39)

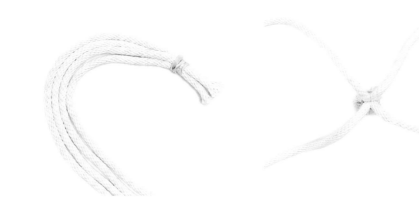

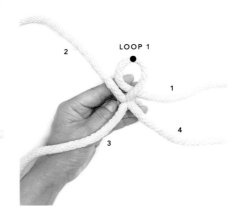

1 Seize the four strands 3″ (7.5 cm) from an end using the rubber band.

2 Despite the accompanying photos, which I've taken on a tabletop to aid in clarity, the easiest way to make the Star Knot is in the hand. Hold the seized ends in the fist, like a flower stem.

3 Arrange the strands equidistant from each other.

4 Form a small loop with cord 1. My method for creating the small loop is to grasp a bit of cord 1 with the fingers of my right hand, then rotate the bit of cord counterclockwise.

The end should emerge from *behind* the loop.

Use the thumb of your stem-grasping hand to press down on the crossing part of loop 1, so it doesn't collapse.

Always work counterclockwise. Turn your attention to cord 2.

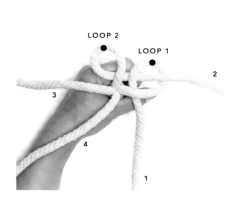

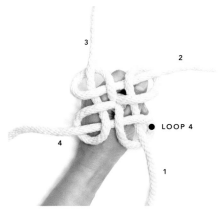

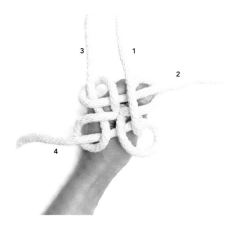

5 Before making a loop in cord 2, lead the end of cord 2 *upward* through loop 1. Pull it almost all the way through.

Then, grasp cord 2 near the knot stem with right hand and turn the bit of cord counter-clockwise. This action will create a loop that should be identical to loop 1 in that the working end of the cord is emerging from *behind* its loop.

6 Repeat the previous step with cords 3 and 4, always first lead-ing the cord up through the previously made loop before forming its own loop.

It helps to use your left thumb to hold down whichever is the most recently made loop, which will serve to hold every-thing else in place, too.

The last step is to feed cord 1 up through loop 4.

Study the photo very carefully and ensure your knot looks like it, especially the over-under crossings.

7 Crown all four cords to the right. (You learned crowning on page 90)

To do this, first lead cord 1 back along itself. In other words, in the previous photo, it was traveling downward, so now it goes upward, and in doing so it crowns cord 2.

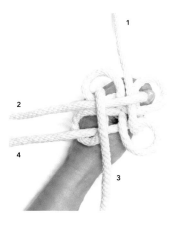

8 As you will recall, to crown is to cross *over* a cord's neighbor.

Here, we see cord 1 has crowned cord 2, cord 2 has crowned cord 3, and cord 3 crowns cord 4.

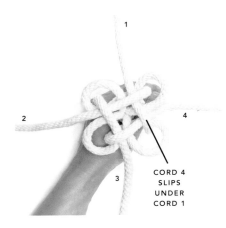

CORD 4
SLIPS
UNDER
CORD 1

9 Last, lead cord 4 to crown cord 1.

Remember that when cord 4 crowns cord 1, it actually must slip *under* the working end of cord 1, as shown.

It took me a while to understand the logic of that concept, but when my fingers made the crown, my eyes understood, because it looked right.

Look at your crown. Notice how the four straight lines form a square in the center of the knot.

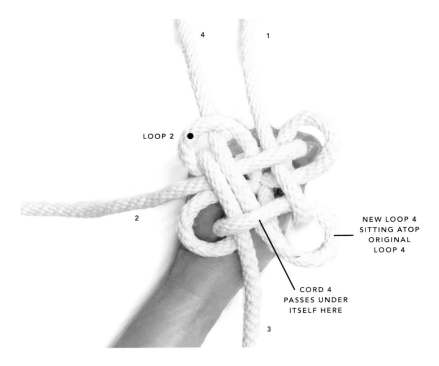

LOOP 2

NEW LOOP 4
SITTING ATOP
ORIGINAL
LOOP 4

CORD 4
PASSES UNDER
ITSELF HERE

10 The next step is to *double* each of the four lines in the square, so it becomes four *pairs* of lines forming the square.

First, grasp any cord. In the photo, I'm working cord 4.

Draw cord 4 to the left toward cord 3, tuck cord 4 under itself to form a loop, then draw it up alongside cord 3, following cord 3 *down into* loop 2. Keep cord 4 on the *inside* of cord 3 (inside meaning closer to the knot center).

In other words, it is a two-part action: First loop the cord under itself, then run it inside and parallel to cord 3 until diving down into loop 2.

While doing this, cord 4 will have made another loop over the first loop 4. Look at loop 4 and notice that there are now two loops in this spot. The new loop might be drooping over the one under it. Adjust the new loop 4 so it is the same size as the original loop 4, and sits atop the original like a pancake.

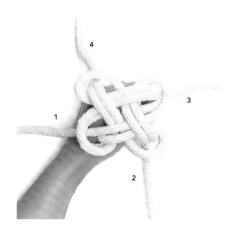

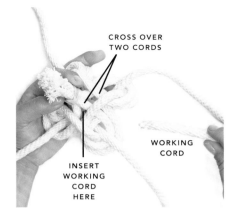

CROSS OVER
TWO CORDS

WORKING
CORD

INSERT
WORKING
CORD
HERE

11 Repeat the identical actions with the remaining three cords, moving clockwise. The only difference is that after the working cord forms a loop and passes under itself, it will also be passing under a *pair* of parallel cords, one of which is itself.

Your square should now be bordered by pairs of lines, as shown. Furthermore, all four of the outer loop shapes should actually be pairs of loops, one loop sitting atop the other, like pancakes.

12 Notice, again, the square-shaped hole in the center of the knot.

If necessary, enlarge it so you can fit two fingers in.

13 Turn the knot over completely, stem pointing up. Notice the square that is surrounding the stem. Looks familiar, right? Similar to what you did with the other square on the top side of the knot, you will be doubling the four lines of this square so that it becomes four *pairs* of lines making the square.

To do this, grasp any one of the working cords. Notice that this working cord is popping up from a loop, along with one of the square's sides. Double the square's side with the working cord, by laying it parallel and on the inside (closer to the stem). You'll be drawing the cord clockwise around the stem.

As you are laying the working cord parallel to the square's side, notice that it *crosses over* two cords (see photo). I find it helpful to count "1 . . . 2 . . ." out loud. After it has passed over two cords, plunge it down *into* the stem and through the knot's square-shaped center hole, out through the other side of the knot.

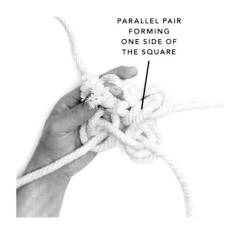

14 From underneath the hole, grab the working cord and pull it all the way through.

If you've done this correctly, you will see a *pair* of parallel cords on one side of the square.

15 Repeat with the three remaining cords.

When this step is completed, you should see a square formed by four *pairs* of parallel cords, just like the one on the top of the knot.

In fact, at this point, the top and the bottom of the knot are identical, with each side showing a square made with parallel pairs of lines.

16 Here's a side view of what the properly made knot looks like thus far.

Four strands should be emerging from the centers of both the top and the bottom of the knot. Around the knot perimeter should be four pairs of petal-like outer loops.

17 Turn the knot right-side up, holding the stem in your fist.

Arrange the cords equidistantly apart.

18 One at a time, draw each cord clockwise and down into a loop, alongside the cord pair that is already going into the loop.

Repeat for each of the four cords.

19 When all four cords are drawn down into the four loops, you will see that you've created what a looks like a triple crown, with three parallel cords entering each loop.

20 We're almost there. Congratulations on getting this far!

Turn the knot facedown again, stem pointing up. One cord should be popping out of each loop.

Notice the square formed by the four pairs of parallel cords surrounding the stem.

The next step is to tuck each of the four cords toward the center under the four sides of the square to join the stem.

multistrand star knot

WORKING CORD
TUCKS *UNDER*
THIS PAIR

WORKING
CORD

21 Grasp one of the cords (it doesn't matter which) and tuck it under the side of the square that is between the working cord and the stem.

Repeat with remaining three cords. Each cord will tuck under a different side of the square.

22 If done correctly, all eight of the ends now should be clustered together.

Remove the rubber band.

Trim the stem ends to 3" (7.5 cm).

23 With the ¼" (6-mm) cord or small stuff, apply the Common Whipping (page 27) to seize together the eight ends. Trim the legs again if they're messy.

24 Here, the finished Star along with a back view and a five-strand version.

today

When I installed the edition of the Year of Knots on a thirty-foot wall at Facebook's campus, I felt thrilled knowing the work would be permanently seen and enjoyed. (Yes, I remade all 366 knots! And should an opportunity present itself, I'll make future editions.) There, **it lives as a document of an incredibly fertile year of learning, growth, and the development of my artistic language.**

However, it was only the beginning of where the knots would take me. In the time since, I've created room-size installations and environments that continue to investigate the potential of the line, and that invite the viewer to activate the space as they move through, under, and past the works. These days, I am contacted daily by new clients, collaborators, and collectors, and more often than not, they want me to propose the art rather than having a preconceived notion of what they desire. They come with an attitude of openness, asking, "What do you think would be good in this space?" It feels like a dream come true: I can make what inspires me.

But the point is, I wouldn't be here, having earned their trust, if I hadn't paid my dues during the Year of Knots. That discipline and rigor and everything that came out of it is how I developed ninja-level expertise. It is this experience, coupled with my aesthetic, that allows me to command a fitting fee and feel great about it.

Today, when I'm asked to make work, I must be consultant, adviser, and director of the work in ways that surpass just the artfulness of the piece. I must think beyond the aesthetic values to cover all the elements that come into play. I am thinking about durability and how the work will age (always a concern with fiber art, because rope expands and contracts with weather and time). I am choosing the appropriate knots carefully, looking for opportunities to make meaning by connecting them with the environment in which they'll be living. If I were creating installations that simply look cool, I wouldn't be doing my job to make art that truly communicates.

The way I think about it, **I now have the knowledge, freedom, permission, and funding to have an idea and follow the line where it wants to go.** Through the Year of Knots, I created my own "master's degree" in how to be a working fine artist. It's like an orchard I planted that keeps bearing fruit. As the physical size of my works has continued to expand, growing bigger than I am, my niece—herself an artist—pointed out that when we make work that is big, then we are inherently *bigger than the work*, because we made it. She's right; I do like my work taking up space. Because I have a lot to say.

The original Year of Knots dominates my studio, sprawling over two walls, and I use those dear knots as my artist palette every day. Whenever I need a new knot to complete a piece, I look up and find the right one.

THE YEAR OF KNOTS *Left to right, across spread*

Left to right, across spread

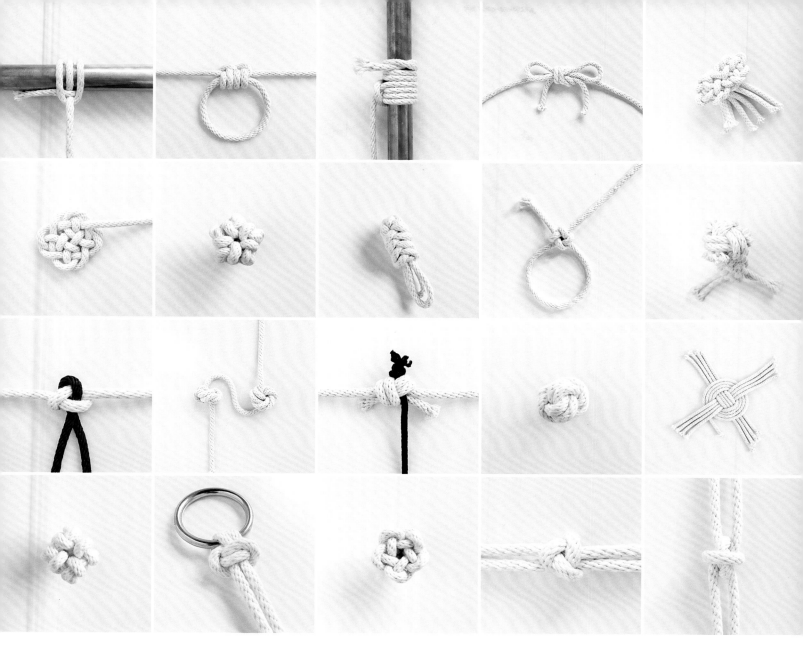

Left to right, across spread

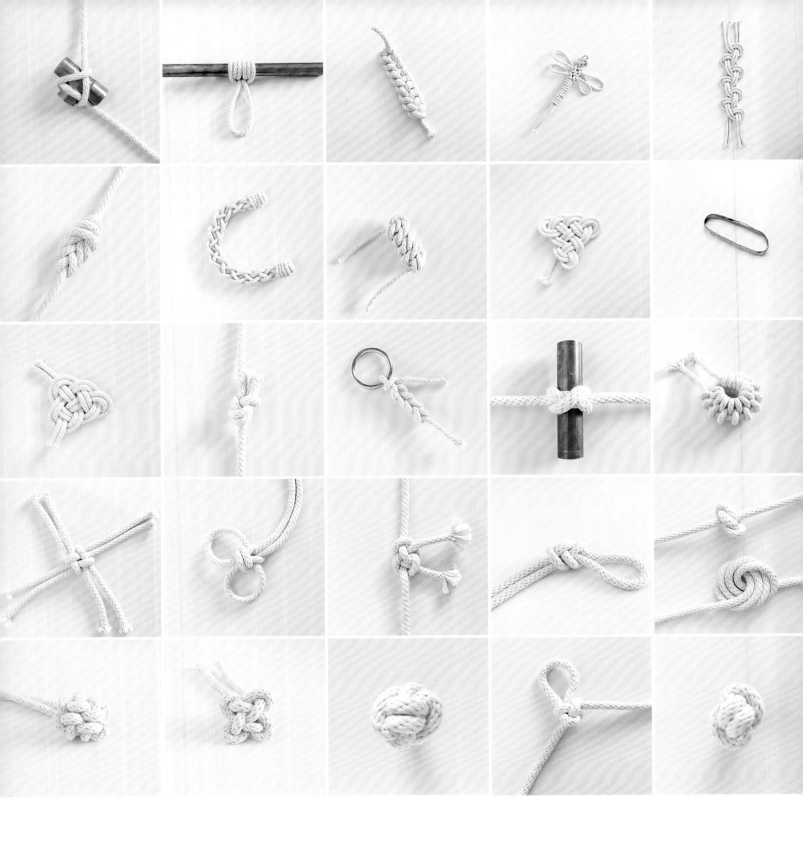

Left to right, across spread

Buoy Rope Hitch
Double Strap Hitch
Figure Eight Chain
The Dragonfly
Double Tatted Chain
'Two Hearts Beat As One' Sheepshank
Pile Hitch
Double Noose
Binding Knot
Granny Knot
Seven-Lead Twist Braid Trumpet Cord
Six-Strand Plat Sinnet

Round Sinnet.
Le Mors du Cheval
The Common Rubber Band
Single-Strand Button Knot
Double Loop
Coachwhipping
Italian Hitch
Anchor Bend
Flat Knot
Double Weaver's Knot
Chain Slipknot
Constrictor Knot

The Cruller
Four-Strand Woven Sinnet
Heaving Line Stopper Knot
Square Loop Sinnet
Chinese Knot
Reef Knot
True Lover's Knot
Double Loop
Bend
Decorative Single Loop Knot
Four-Ply Single-Strand Lanyard Knot
Single Loop Knot

Slipped Post Hitch
Double Parallel Loop Knot
Multiple Loop Knot
English Cringle
Single-Strand Button Knot
Square Button Knot
Single-Strand Button
Loop Knot in the Bight
Single-Strand Button

Left to right, across spread

Single-Strand Button Knot
Grapevine Knot
Shroud Knot Tassel
Hitch
Grog's Sliding Splice
The Ashley Bend
Thumb Knot
Single-Strand Button from Loop Knot
Three-Strand Double Wall Stopper Knot
Capt. Albert Whitney's Six-Strand Sinnet
Diamond Ring Knot
Bowline in the Bight

Monkey Chain
Gibbet Knot
Scout Coil
Bunny Ears
Bimini Twist
Double Diamond
Multi-Strand Diamond Knot
Snaking
Korean Ring Knots
Ginger Knot
Spectacle (Plafond) Knot
Chain Sinnet

Two-Ring Monkey's Fist
Rib Stitch Hitching
Chinese Butterfly Knot
Flat Knot Medallion
Five-Bight Single-Cord Lanyard
Double Crown Knot
The Tweenie
Flat Knot Medallion
Three-Strand Button
Rectangular Knot
Flat Knot Medallion
Flat Monkey's Fist

Decorative Flat Knot
Japanese Parcel Knot, Gift Knot variant
Clove Hitches
Single Genoese Bar
Kellig Hitch
Double Loop Knot
Single Cat's Paw
Triangular Crown Sinnet
Boom Stopper Knot

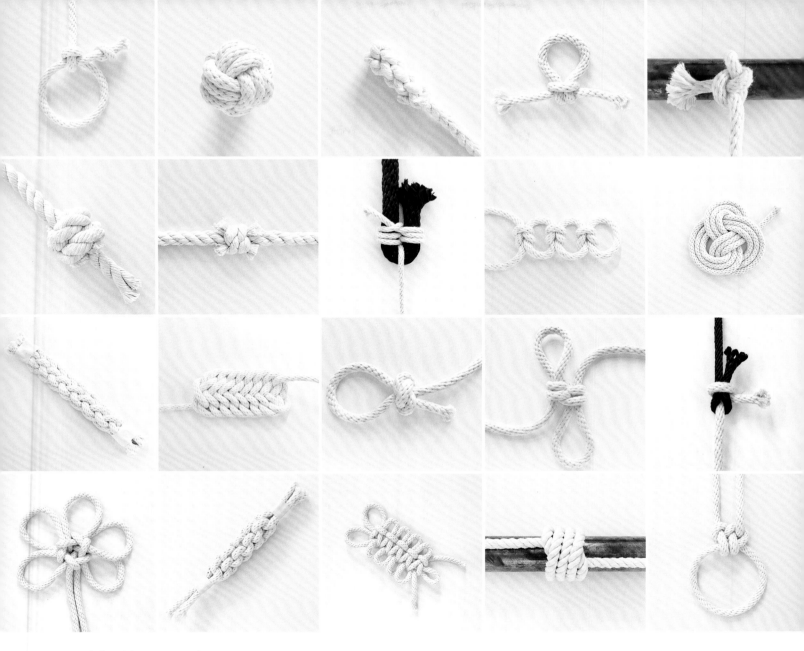

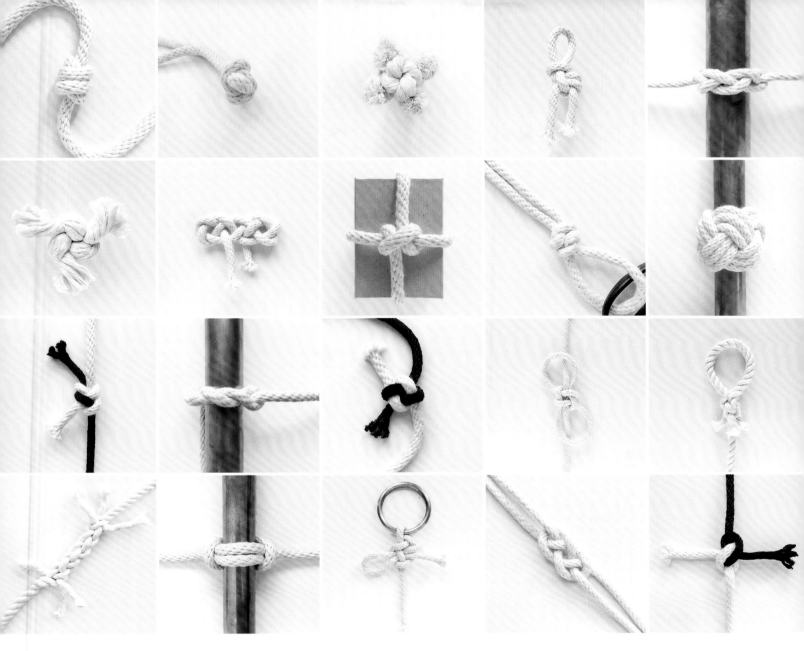

Left to right, across spread

Double Loop
Buttonhole Bar
Five-Strand Star Knot
Overhand Loop
Four-Strand Rectangular Button Knot
Threefold Overhand Knot
Two-Bight, One Lead Turk's Head Button
Multi-Strand Lanyard Knot
Single Loop Knot
Snug Hitch
Wall Sinnet
Crossing Knot

Doubled Eight-Part Single-Strand Button
Chain Sinnet
Matthew Walker Knot
Multi-Strand Stopper Knot
Rectangular Knot
Clove Hitch
Englishman's Loop
Single-Strand Turk's Head
Flat Single-Strand Turk's Head
Half-Hitched Half Hitch
Basket Weave Knot
Two-Strand Lanyard Knot

Two-Strand Flat Lanyard Knot
Jamming Bend
Timber Hitch
Japanese Bend
Lanyard Knot with square crown
Sailor's Eye Splice
Butterfly Knot with triangular crown
Flemish Flake
Six-Strand French Sinnet
Corkscrew Bar
Oysterman's Knot
Sailor's Short Splice

Crossing Hitch
Sampan Hitch
Josephine Knot
Hunter's Bend
Tag Knot
Studding-Sail Bend
The Angler's Loop
Single-Strand Stopper Knot
True Lovers Knot

187

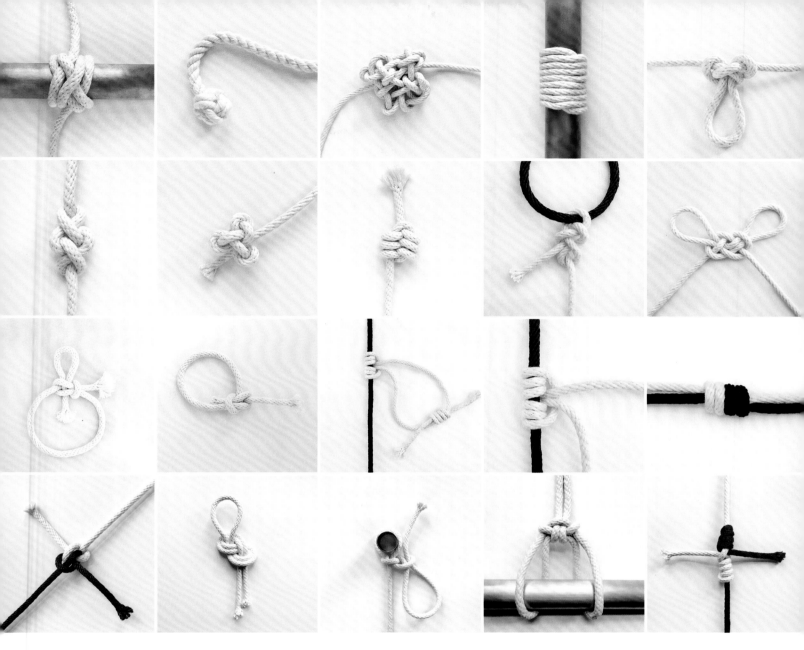

Left to right, across spread

Gary L. Baker II, until I met you, I didn't believe a relationship like ours was possible, yet here you are: my best friend and most trusted adviser. You see the big picture and find the truth in every instance, and in doing so you bring my life into focus. In short, this book wouldn't have happened without you. Thank you, my love.

Thank you, Jamie Shaw, for your way with words, your insights and wisdom, and for somehow knowing the right combination of wine and food to draw all the stories out of me.

Vero Kherian, you shoot white on white better than anyone. I'm happy to have the chance to grow and create together with you. Thank you for your patience, hard work, and expertise while photographing the knot lessons in this book.

Thanks to my publishing A-team for your kindness, wisdom, and advocacy: agent Jen Marshall, editor and editorial director Shawna Mullen, designers Deb Wood and Heesang Lee, Marisa Meltzer, and the good people of Abrams and Aevitas Creative Management. Your guidance was invaluable in the creation of this book.

Cesar Rubio, I am grateful for your photographs, which make me see my work with fresh eyes. For this incredible support, I thank you, dear friend.

Hannah Lew, my rescuer, girlfriend, confidante, and inspiration: thank you.

Marie Muscardini, thank you for providing a home for artists in the Bay Area, and for showing me I could become a teacher.

Thank you, Katie Geminder, for creating a retreat for artists on your magical Bolinas property.

Thanks to my talented photographer friends spread all over the country, Lexi Ribar and Leslie Santarina, and to Samantha Altieri, Molly DeCoudreaux, Daniel Green, Peter Prato, and Anthony Strong, whose photos appear in this book.

To my professional sisters who provide the kind of expertise that allows me to keep going, thank you, Constance Young, Nina Kaufman, and Heather Marie English. And especially to Melissa Davis: thank you for helping me see myself, and for bringing me to the next level.

Artist friends Isobel Schofield, Katie Gong: thank you for the opportunity to collaborate with you. I'm proud of the works we made together and thrilled to include them in this book.

Brianna Applegate, Chris Brown, Alisa Carroll, Ashley Cunningham, John Darnielle, Cathy Fitzhugh, Lan-Chi Lam, Marialidia Marcotulli, David Sams, Loren Skelly, Noel Tolentino, Anastasia Tumanova, and Tiffanie Vo all pitched in to bring this book to life: Thank you.

To my Instagram community who were with me every day of the year: thank you.

To the Bay Area community of female founders, entrepreneurs, writers, photographers, artists, doers, thinkers, and makers, I'm so glad we can support one another. Thank you.

Thanks, Dad, for passing on your perfect design sense and setting a good example of using one's hands to create.

And finally, Mom, thanks for teaching me macramé when I was a child. Good thing you did! I love you.

acknowledgments

Praise for *The Year of Knots*

"Windy Chien always jokes she had three lives: running a rad record store, working for Apple, and finally . . . creating art with rope. Windy is a real inspiration, for not only taking a big risk to follow her true path, but using her past to create a brand in almost the snap of her fingers, or the twist of a knot!"

CINDY ALLEN, editor in chief, *Interior Design*

"*The Year of Knots* is a testament to Windy's unbridled commitment to her craft and, in turn, a generous and enduring gift to us all."

ERICA CHAN COFFMAN, HonestlyWTF